Meeting Management

Taggart E. Smith, Ph.D.

Purdue University

Management Skills
NetEffect Series

Prentice
Hall

Upper Saddle River, New Jersey 07458

Library of Congress Cataloging-in-Publication Data

Smith, Taggart.
    Meeting management / Taggart Smith.
        p.   cm.
    Includes bibliographical references and index.
    ISBN 0–13–017391–6
    1. Meetings.   2. Business communication.   I. Title.
    HF5718.T34   2000
    658.4′56—dc
                                                  00-055732

Executive Editor: *Elizabeth Sugg*
Editorial Assistant: *Anita Rhodes*
Director of Manufacturing and Production: *Bruce Johnson*
Managing Production Editor: *Mary Carnis*
Production Editor: *Kristen Butler, BookMasters, Inc.*
Production Liaison: *Eileen O'Sullivan*
Manufacturing Manager: *Ed O'Dougherty*
Cover Illustration: *Tom White*
Cover Design: *Lafortezza Design Group*
Composition: *BookMasters, Inc.*
Printing and Binding: *R.R. Donnelley & Sons, Harrisonburg, VA*

Prentice-Hall International (UK) Limited, *London*
Prentice-Hall of Australia Pty, Limited, *Sydney*
Prentice-Hall Canada, Inc., *Toronto*
Prentice-Hall Hispanoamericana, S.A., *Mexico*
Prentice-Hall of India Private Limited, *New Delhi*
Prentice-Hall of Japan, Inc., *Tokyo*
Prentice-Hall Singapore Pte. Ltd.
Editora Prentice-Hall do Brasil Ltda., *Rio de Janeiro*

10 9 8 7 6 5 4 3 2 1
ISBN 0-13-017391-6

Dedication

Thanks to all the Purdue students who have taken conference leadership in past years. Many of the ideas in this book, as well as the need for a book, came from you. Working with bright minds, quick senses of humor, and an infinity of new ways to do things is a constant pleasure in teaching. Thanks for being you.

Taggart Smith

Contents

8   **CONDUCTING DECISION-MAKING MEETINGS**   **85**

Preface

Behavioral scientists have been studying how to make meetings more effective for decades. This book is not necessarily a breakthrough in this study, but it does offer an applied framework for managing meetings, rather than a theoretical one. One thing is certain: Quality of leadership is an important determinant of meeting success.

Conducting a meeting is a difficult job, because groups want leaders with just the right balance between "taking charge" and "letting go." Leaders who are too dominant or too passive will have ineffective group meetings. An effective leader balances process control and content control, which requires considerable skill. Meetings function as information-processing systems in organizations. In good meetings, issues are fully discussed, decisions are well considered and need no rework, and participants feel good about participating. A meeting leader, then, is responsible for the contribution of information and ideas by group members, the clarity of communication, the focus of discussion, and the resolution of disagreement. There are ways to plan and conduct meetings that accomplish these purposes, and that is where this book comes in.

Chapters 1, 2, and 3 show how to organize and present information-giving meetings. Everything from outlining key points, maintaining interest, using visuals, and employing nonverbal communication is addressed. Chapters 4, 5, and 6 prepare leaders for interactive meetings. Here leaders learn when to have meetings, why they are necessary, what roles are recommended, and how to deal with classic problems of meeting disruptions. Chapter 7 examines problem-solving meetings in depth and features some examples and a practice exercise. Chapter 8 offers details on conducting discussions with special emphasis on asking questions and gaining consensus in groups. A method of determining the best solutions to problems is described using construction of criteria for judging different alternatives.

For each of these three meetings, content outlines are provided, along with critique sheets and observation sheets. Again, the emphasis here is application oriented. These outlines provide ways to process information in organizations, to solve problems using group input, and to decide the best way to proceed when solutions are found. During the learning process, leaders find their strengths and weaknesses and practice getting groups to respond efficiently and effectively.

The material for this book evolved from a business administration curriculum at Purdue University. The book emerged over time and in response to the expressed needs of students as they honed their meeting management skills. Thus, the "best and the brightest," in this author's opinion, created this book.

In summary, the study of managing meetings has been going on for some time—and continues still. This book attempts to put a practical face on the problem of leading meetings effectively and efficiently. Just as we never outgrow our need for milk, at least according to current advertising, we never outgrow our need for efficient meetings. Even in this age of continuous innovation in communication, we still need face-to-face meetings to make quality decisions.

Jeff Bezos, Amazon.com's chief, in an interview for the *Wall Street Journal*, had this to say:

WSJ: How do you work with your directors? Something tells me this isn't quite like U.S. Steel in the 1920s, with a long mahogany table and six-hour board meetings.

BEZOS: We're actually a little old-fashioned in this respect. There's nothing better than an in-person meeting. Nothing yet has replicated that, as far as I know. For quick interaction, e-mail and phone are great. But for really getting into something, a physical meeting is much better. We laugh a lot at our board meetings—and we get a lot done. (*Wall Street Journal*, February 4, 2000, pp. B1–B4.)

If Mr. Dot Com himself considers meetings important, so should we.

Acknowledgments

We would like to thank these experts for their valuable advice:

1. Virginia Dumont-Poston, Lander University
2. Katherine H. Isenburg, Indian River Community College
3. Estelle Kochis, Suffolk Community College
4. Jo Ann Mitchell, University of Southern Mississippi

Overview of the Meeting Process

Introduction

Dwight Lee and Richard McKenzie, authors of *Getting Rich in America* (1999), have this advice concerning schooling: your goal should be to discover not only what is financially rewarding, but also intellectually satisfying to you. How do you do that?

1. Select a wide range of academic topics, thus increasing your choices for career paths.
2. Remember that broad education produces well-rounded employees with the versatility to advance in organizations.
3. Take advantage of specialized training employers offer.

What sorts of graduates are hired? These employers hire those with good general education and efficient learning skills as evidenced by degree completion, good grades, and well-chosen coursework. A further hiring factor is the peer group or cohort with whom students associate while in school. To complete a degree in the company of those who compete, cooperate, and thrive in the zeitgeist of college years is a mark of achievement. Showing the ability to influence and lead that cohort group produces an even stronger track record.

How do you favorably influence your peer group before or after graduation?

Interacting in groups and organizations

Showing the ability to work hard

Demonstrating trustworthiness

Impressing these attributes on an increasing network of people

What arena provides an opportunity to showcase these attributes? Meeting management!

Think about it: few people see you at your desk writing reports or telephoning or using your computer productively. They do see the results of these activities, but it's hard to ascribe leadership capability to a desk-sitter. To be perceived as a competent,

1

capable leader on a campus or in an organization, you need to leave your desk and get in front of a group, leading them to do something worthwhile. Managing meetings is definitely a step in the right direction.

Importance of Meeting Management

How important is it to manage meetings efficiently? *Some estimates of time spent in business meetings range from 40 to 60 percent.* Nearly half of most managers' work hours are spent in meetings! What are the usual complaints about meetings? "Boring!" "Off the topic!" "Waste of time!" Most of us have endured poorly run meetings in which the communication goes in circles, and nothing is accomplished. Yet, how much time, energy, and money do we spend meeting? Most organizations spend between 7 and 15 percent of personnel budgets on meetings. Community groups are literally run by meetings. Much of this effort may be volunteer, so there may not be a monetary cost, but there is a time cost, and time is a valuable resource to most people. Let's look at time spent at work.

In essence, if you have a paying job, you rent out a certain number of hours of your daily life to your employer. Your employer expects a certain amount of accomplishment during those hours, given your training and work ethic. As an employee, you expect management to supply the necessary resources you need to accomplish your work: adequate supplies, equipment in good working order, guidance in how the company wants the work done, and an evaluation procedure to tell when you succeed or fail.

Where does meeting management fall in all this? After all, don't most people know how to communicate? Isn't it logical to assume that if people know how to talk to one another, groups of people ought to be able to get together, come to decisions, and go on with their other work? Besides, email messaging and chat rooms are available now; maybe we don't even need meetings anymore. The end result is using human communication skills productively in the work environment. Granted, we can reduce communication to its lowest common denominator through this thinking. However, this thought pattern fails to recognize the complexity of human beings and our society. A key word in the end result statement is "productively." Many meetings *are* unnecessary, for example when things could be accomplished through other means, there's no reason to meet, the wrong people attend, or there's not enough time to prepare properly. In these instances, spare everyone and don't have a meeting.

On the other hand, most organizations couldn't function without meetings. Across America, leaders are guiding small groups of people through the process of communicating in a limited time frame. People have to communicate in groups to get things done. Sitting down face to face with group members is an effective way to accomplish tasks. When people gather to communicate, they can react to others' comments, ask questions, voice arguments, process information, and ultimately produce better decisions. They can pool their knowledge and experiences, so that the group becomes more than the sum of its parts.

A further plus for quality meetings is that they meet workers' needs for feeling part of a group or being a team member. People have a need for togetherness, trust, and belonging, and the meeting process fosters this. In today's cubically-organized and computer-oriented work world, meetings ease loneliness and help distribute the workload. Effective meetings help develop a sense of commitment to organizations, as well as a feeling of contributing solutions to a problem—a sense of having accomplished something worthwhile. Even if solutions proposed are not what all group members originally supported, at least they feel "heard" through the process and are more likely to support the solution selected after group deliberation. Sometimes meetings provide the only time members see themselves as a group. With flexible hours, varying work shifts, telecommuting, and persons essentially operating as solo units of responsibility especially in government and higher education organizations, group experiences affect how people feel about their organization. Meetings also have a ripple effect throughout organizations in that one manager or faculty member or GS 7 government employee returning from a frustrating time *or* a well-orchestrated event may impact 15 other managers, 30 students in a classroom, or a 50-person department. Thus, meetings can be tremendously positive or negative in organizations. Improving meetings can improve not only communication, but also morale and productivity in the workforce.

An added benefit to learning to conduct efficient and effective meetings is the benefit to your image. When others see you "in action" in meetings, they form opinions about your competence based on what they see and hear. If you are able to sift information to find the issues that matter, get groups to deliberate these issues, and get consensus on decisions with these issues, you can become known as a skillful leader. Another consideration which should interest you is that leading a group—that is, determining meeting process and content—is very powerful. If you can control the process—who speaks, how long they can speak, guiding decision making, and summarizing—you can determine to a large extent what happens. Process can control content, and that's the *core of meeting management.* Once you learn how to manage meetings, you can manage them anywhere: churches, homes, support groups, neighborhood associations, youth groups, civic organizations, as well as your workplace. Key to good management is preparing for meetings. In this book, you will find guidance on organizing your message and presenting it effectively, so that people listen and are persuaded by your words and your presence. You will learn how to conduct information-giving, problem-solving, and decision-making meetings. The structure provided is one you can take anywhere and adapt to your setting.

Structure for Three Types of Meetings

Normally, of course, these three segments might occur in one meeting, depending on the issues involved. Here, however, the three meeting types are considered separately in order to bring out instructional details inherent in each type. In the first meeting described, you will learn presentation skills, structuring information for an oral delivery, and writing a meeting agenda, including a meeting objective. In the problem-solving instruction, you will learn more about planning an interactive meeting, delegating meeting roles for those in attendance, and influencing groups. In the decision-making meeting, you will learn how to frame a decision so that a problem can be examined from several angles, establish criteria for quality decisions, and deal with various types of people who impede the meeting process. You'll be given guidelines for performance in each meeting type, plus observer sheets and critique forms. Since efficiency is a concern along with effectiveness, limit information meetings to *ten* minutes, problem solving to *twenty* minutes, and decision making to *thirty* minutes.

For fast improvement, videotape yourself conducting meetings. Initially people balk at this, but most literally see the benefit. This will teach you more than any other thing about your effectiveness as a meeting leader. Most people discover that they come across far better externally than they felt internally during a videotaped meeting. Remember that you're not trying for broadcast quality performances here! You're using a feedback technique for self-improvement. An interesting closure step after completing the three segments is to view your videotape in one sitting. You'll be amazed at your improvement! A comment form to solemnize your achievement is included.

The meeting process described here has been field tested for a number of years with students at Purdue University. Their comments and feedback have been incorporated into this text and the methods presented here. Their classroom performances have improved incrementally as they developed into public speakers and meeting leaders. Invariably, near the end of this coursework, students smile more and act very much at ease during their meetings. A standard answer on a class evaluation question, "What will you take with you from this course?" is this: *"I feel so good knowing how to set up meetings and then carry them out. I'm really confident I'll be able to do this well in the future."* And so will you!

In summary, then, we've established that students should get a broad education as well as having a specialty area to be a well-rounded employee. Employers look for evidence of your ability to lead, which you can show through meeting management. Meetings are important to organizations and give company-wide notice of your professional competence. This book illustrates three types of meetings: information giving, problem solving, and decision making.

Selecting a Topic

Some readers of this book will have built-in opportunities to practice the techniques and methods detailed here. If you are the presiding officer of a club, chairing a committee, managing a business, or pastoring a church, you have issues and opportunities to try out these guidelines for managing meetings. If you already have issues, use them. However, if you want to practice a bit before trying your "meeting wings," select a topic to use in working through the three meeting segments detailed in this book. In general, this section will help crystallize your thinking about the process used in setting up meetings.

Information Meeting Considerations

You need a topic on which you can find enough material to present a fairly detailed ten-minute information meeting. The material needs to divide logically into three major areas for the purposes of your first presentation. Then, consider what problem lies in this topic, since you'll have to parlay your information into a problem-solving format for the second segment. The third segment, decision making, is a matter of choosing among alternatives developed in the problem-solving meeting, so this segment doesn't play into your choice of topics quite so much. Remember that the major input of information comes during your first meeting, but you need to know enough about your topic to answer whatever questions may occur during problem solving and decision making. In the last two meetings, you basically introduce yourself and repeat the highlights of your information talk, but the structure in the last two meetings usually requires a major portion of time. It is nice to "freshen" your material with a new fact or two!

A caveat, however, is not to select a topic in which choices are limited.

Problem-Solving Tips

For example, the quandary of whether to lease or buy a vehicle sometimes arises. Could you gather enough material for a ten-minute information meeting? Yes. What problem within the topic would you attempt to solve? An obvious strategy is to make one pro-and-con list for buying, and one pro-and-con list for leasing. Several problems are inherent in this topic choice.

The goal of your problem-solving meeting is to have a group of participants collaborate to construct a list of alternatives which could solve the problem you've advanced. As a topic, buying or leasing a car only provides two alternatives. The instructional process used here requires at least five viable alternatives, so unless you can think of a way to stretch buy or lease into five different alternatives, this topic won't work. Buying or leasing is more of a personal choice issue, rather than one which requires group discussion and decision making. So your challenge is to find a topic in which there is a problem which a group can discuss and on which consensus is possible.

Another reason not to use this particular topic is the problem you create for participants. In your first meeting, you hold forth for ten minutes about the advantages and disadvantages of buying versus leasing. If you start a problem-solving meeting on this, you will essentially be asking participants to list back for you the information you gave out in your first meeting. Wait a minute! You're supposed to be the expert on this topic, not the audience! Don't make problem solving into a reverberation of an information meeting.

What you're aiming for in problem solving *and* decision making is to encourage discussion from several points of view. You're trying to elicit other people's ideas. "Here's what I know. Now, tell me what you think."

Let's take another example. If you've selected fire safety in the home as your topic, your three main points could include:

1. the prevalence of home fires and damages to life and property
2. precautions to observe in preventing home fires
3. equipment/devices that homeowners should have and maintain

This is a lot of information for a ten-minute talk, but it can be done if you are succinct and well-organized. Where's the problem to be solved? You don't want to ask participants to list ways to prevent fires, because that's what you told them earlier. If in your first talk you mentioned smoke alarms as useful devices, in your problem-solving talk you could ask people to brainstorm ways to encourage the use of home smoke alarms. During the problem-solving meeting participants might respond with these ideas:

- hand out alarms free during Fire Prevention Week
- have volunteer firefighters install alarms for purchasers
- ask local government to subsidize their purchase in high-risk areas
- reduce property tax rates if alarms are in place
- lobby for a local ordinance requiring their use

And the list goes on! This is the purpose of a problem-solving meeting—having people brainstorm possible solutions to the problem you've posed. In decision making, then, you can list the five alternatives arrived at previously and ask the audience to select the best alternative.

Notice in the fire safety example that smoke alarms came from the third main point of the first meeting. Frequently, choosing an item imbedded in a main point as a problem to solve is good and a natural thought progression for your audience. Remember, it always has to make sense to them. Thus, the idea here is to choose a topic with an imbedded problem in mind.

Your question now probably is: Can I just talk about a problem to begin with and then solve it? The answer is, "Yes, but. . . ." If the problem is a terribly complex one in which a number of issues need to be fleshed out thoroughly, you may need the ten-minute information meeting to make participants aware of everything they need to consider. Topics we've used in class which fit this description: introducing and encouraging Euro currency use in geographically remote areas of Europe; ameliorating the cultural disputes in northern Ireland; and addressing individual rights issues in the Kashmir/Pakistan conflict. These topics were very good ones, but they demanded a higher level of information sifting and presenting from the students explaining the issues to the class. For the purpose of learning this meeting process, a less complicated topic might be a better choice.

Theory Versus Practice

Now a caveat about selecting too broad a topic! Let's say you've just gotten a directive from upper management to make your work group aware of sexual harassment. Is this topic too broad for a ten-minute meeting? Maybe. The best you could probably do here would be to cover this topic at the theoretical level in a ten-minute talk. Because this is a size Large topic to begin with, the most you could expect would be to define harassment, cite recent court cases, and state your company guidelines on harassment.

This is a problem that needs more specific applications in order to appeal to and become more understandable to most workforces. If you think about it, the function of middle- and first-level managers is to interpret upper-level management pronouncements to the rest of the workforce. So, if you just define harassment and say, "Don't do it," will that take care of the matter for workers? Probably not. The theory isn't translated into practice, and to change behavior, we all need practice— albeit theory-based.

Your problem-solving meeting would have to be at the theoretical level as well. You'd probably ask the group to brainstorm ideas for preventing harassment in the workplace. Ideas advanced might be:

- a hands-off rule for all work areas
- a clearly defined policy from management
- training for all supervisors
- an anonymous reporting system for violations
- zero tolerance for infractions

This is not a bad list; in several respects, it is good. The point here is that these alternatives are more theory than practice. These are alternatives you could probably find in a textbook on the subject. What brainstorming at this level will produce are textbook answers to harassment problems. Does this solve problems? Yes, but if theory isn't interpreted in the light of practicality, what good will it do toward changing people's behavior?

Will people in the workforce change their behavior on Monday morning as a result of having this meeting on Friday afternoon? Looking at the alternatives generated in the last example, the onus for change lies primarily with management. Drawing up a statement on harassment, setting up a reporting hotline, or establishing a hands-off rule are management responsibilities. If you are having a meeting of managers, this would be fine. If you're having a meeting of workers, this doesn't give them the substance they need to change their behavior. One way of determining whether learning has occurred is to note whether people change their behavior. The focus in problem solving on this issue needs to be on changing behavior. Perhaps asking them to recount critical incidents they've seen, or posing a situation and asking for input, or conducting a role play would be better ideas for meetings of this nature. So, a better problem-solving discussion here would center on actualities in the workplace, not theoretical concerns.

The problem reflected here is lack of focus, which is a universal problem with meetings in general. If you want a theory-based outcome, plan for that. If you want a practical outcome, plan for that. Think beyond, "I need to have a meeting," to "What do I want to accomplish with this meeting?" This becomes your meeting objective: why have this meeting. What do you want people to do differently as a result of attending your meeting? More on this later, but for now, choose a topic which is not so broad that all participants can logically arrive at are hackneyed phrases and rule-of-thumb answers. Find something people can get into mentally and emotionally and discuss with fervor.

For example, a subset of the topic of sexual harassment is same-sex harassment— a smaller topic within the broader one. Give some recent examples, something from current news, and ask the audience to create a list of ways to counteract the specific incidences. The idea here is to get concrete, concise recommendations because that's where the workforce lives and functions. This is not a matter of intelligence, because savvy managers know that a lot of very clever people are in the workforce. They are clever in ways that managers aren't, and their skills are needed to produce the product or service of the organization. However, if management is prescribing an atmosphere it wishes to become pervasive or if it is establishing a work rule that all employees are to observe, management should supply guidance as to how work should be done and under what conditions it should be done, which in this example is harassment-free.

That's one of the reasons learning to focus meetings is important. Another, for the purpose of this instruction, is to provide practice in conducting meetings in which heartfelt ideas are discussed. When meetings center on real issues, they are meaningful and worthwhile.

A final bit of advice on meeting topics. Choose something you care about. It's hard to be enthusiastic about a topic when you're thinking, "Frankly, Scarlett. . . ." Half the battle in presenting well and conducting a well-organized meeting is enthusiasm for what you're doing. Choose something that makes your heart beat faster. If nothing comes to mind, read a newspaper, watch a news telecast, or get on the Internet to discover what other people find interesting—within reason, of course. Some issues reflected in recent news:

- ***rating systems for rock concerts***
  Do students and parents need/want parental advisories based on lyrics, stage behavior, or programming at celebrity concerts?

- ***violence in films and media***
  Is the Motion Picture Association of America rating system outdated? Is it important to enforce viewing rules?

- ***college students as credit card targets***
  The Consumers Union is concerned about aggressive marketing of credit cards on campus. Debt has been linked to suicides, dropouts, reduced course loads, and low grades by students working to pay off credit card debt. Are they being unfairly targeted?

- ***boorish behavior versus freedom of speech***
  In central Michigan, government officials, canoe outfitters, and the general public are standing up for civility by launching a decorum campaign. The issue is protecting families, especially young children, from rude language and behavior. Does this impinge on free speech?

These are newsprint articles only, so to develop your topic, you'd need to find more information from other sources—books, journals, magazines, the Internet, personal experience, interviews with experts, and so on. The worst mistake you can make is not having enough material. Too much material is far better. If you can't work all of it into your information meeting, you can freshen up your information in the problem-solving and decision-making meetings. If you do enough information gathering now, your later meetings will be richer and fuller because you know more and feel good about that!

TOPIC SUGGESTIONS

- Attention deficit disorder or other disorders interfering with performance
- Eating red meat or the value of vegetarianism
- Youth in the labor movement or the usefulness of labor unions today
- College-age voter apathy
- Soda consumption versus calcium needs or soda effect on teeth
- Maintaining interest in 4H, especially older adolescents
- Rights of smokers versus nonsmokers
- Women in combat in military services
- Animal cruelty, especially involving betting
- Missing blood donors or organ donors
- Unsafe sex at college
- AIDS in the workplace or declining media attention to AIDS
- Alternative medicine, safety and practice
- Performance-enhancing drug use among athletes
- Daycare, home versus business, or selecting a daycare service
- Choosing the best company for your first job
- Revenue-producing sports versus non-revenue-producing sports in school
- Sports equipment safety—skiing, biking, rollerblading, etc.
- Divorce after six months or after 25 years
- Increase in obesity
- Managing Internet use in the workplace
- Euthanasia when quality of life is gone

In summary, the format for instruction in this book concerns managing three types of meetings: an information meeting, a problem-solving meeting in which you profile a problem and ask participants to brainstorm solutions, and a decision-making meeting in which you select one solution as the best. Topic choice needs to have a problem imbedded in it, usually something from one of your three major points. Choose a topic you're interested in or other people are interested in—an open-ended problem, one on which people can form opinions and do justice to brainstorming alternatives. Be as specific as possible and aim for a practical outcome as the end result of this meeting process—a behavior-changing choice.

2
Organizing Your Message

Good meetings don't just happen. More preparation goes into "seamless" meetings than you can imagine. This chapter will guide you in spending energy on the right activities. A singular key to effective meetings is preparing an agenda and circulating it in advance—three days before your meeting if possible. When participants have advance agendas, you can expect them to show up on time, bring material relevant to the meeting, and be prepared to do what you've set up as the purpose of your meeting. An hour of preparation on your part can save several hours of actual meeting time, so get set for the pure gratitude of participants when you execute a productive meeting. There's nothing sweeter than to have several people approach you afterward to say, "That was a really good meeting!"

Audience

First consider the people attending your meeting. It's not enough to plan from your perspective alone, since each of us "sees" differently. Plus, if your intent is to deliver a message or solve problems, you need to adopt a relational approach. You're not just talking to folks; you're *relating* with them. You're trying to understand where they are coming from so that you can link with their ideas and feelings, at least enough to get your point across if not persuade them to your way of thinking.

People forget 75 percent of what they hear in 48 hours

UNLESS

meetings are memorable and meaningful!!!

In planning, you need to think from the other side of your desk and deliver your talk or conduct your meeting with listeners' viewpoints in mind. Here is information you should know about your audience before you convene a meeting.

- *Gender and age.*   You might not do anything differently if the audience was largely male or female, but your supporting material could be slanted toward either. Age could make a difference though; talking with retirees or elementary age children would require different focuses. If the crowd is mixed, try to tailor a few remarks to each.

- *Education, job/profession.*   High school graduates and Masters level people would hear you quite differently, as would nurses and retail workers, to name a few. Again, if these are attending a PTA meeting which you are planning to address, be aware of the level of language you use and aim for the middle ground.

- *Setting.*   Small groups behave differently from large ones. Sitting at a table on a dais calls for adjustments as much as having a meeting "in the round" with people surrounding you. Checking for AV equipment ahead of time is a good idea. Addressing "suits" is different from addressing a college crowd.

- *Expectations.*   Does the crowd want entertainment or some serious thoughts? Is this more or less a social gathering, or will the group break into smaller groups and discuss what you said? Are you team-building (rah!) or are you telling folks the plant is closing?

Now comes the hard part! You have to ask yourself what this group would consider important—and plan your meeting from that direction. Empathizing with your audience, walking around in their moccasins for a while, will help you get into their mindsets. What questions are they likely to ask? Get answers in advance; include them in your talk if you prefer. How can you make your message memorable? Even if you're planning meetings for a small work group you know, think about the issues you're bringing up and how they are likely to respond. Open your meeting by asking them what they want to know, and then provide the answers you've prepared. Listen attentively to their problem-solving suggestions, and treat them with respect and courtesy in decision making. Buy a new outfit for the "Great Boss" award ceremony.

Agendas and Meeting Objectives

Now that we know with whom we're doing business, let's structure the meeting. Do this by making an agenda for every meeting you conduct—every meeting. Don't think you don't have time; you will waste more time in a meeting without an agenda than you'll spend constructing one. Agendas help you crystallize your thoughts, as well as provide some direction for the folks attending your meeting.

People want to know what to expect in advance. Don't call meetings unless they are necessary; when they are, let people know what your meeting is about by circulating the agenda at least three days in advance. Then show up on time, keep to the agenda time limits, follow up on responsibilities, and watch your popularity index climb!

In the sample agenda form provided, the first line asks for a meeting objective. **Simply stated, why are you having this meeting?** Why is it important? What's in it for the attendees? Write your meeting objective by answering the question, "During this meeting or when it's over, what do I want people to do?" This objective and your thinking behind it will determine whether your meeting is worth attending! People tend to gloss over this part of planning because they have a mental picture of their topic and what should happen. The problem is that the audience doesn't know all that.

Be specific. Use action verbs, such as to identify, to analyze, to select. Be as concise as you can be. However, don't settle for "to inform about gun control," when you could use "to illustrate loopholes in the law concerning gun ownership" or, "to assess parental responsibility when minors use guns."

So, you've thought long and hard about the meeting objective and have developed one that will accomplish results: information will be imparted or exchanged; plans will be formed; ideas or opinions will be expressed; or decisions will be made. **The objective determines the content of the meeting at the appropriate level of detail.**

AGENDA FOR INFORMATION MEETING

Meeting Objective:

Logistics	*Meeting Members*
Date:	1. Leader:
Time:	2. Attendees:
Location:	Meeting called by:
	Phone:

Agenda Item	Process	Time	Who's Responsible

Sequencing Agenda Items

Next, let's look at the agenda items. These can be sequenced in several ways. Some experts advise starting with the most important items first, when interest and attention are at their highest levels. Some advise handling short, urgent items first so they don't get crowded out of the meeting. Others advise starting with the least important items and ending with the most important, after a working cohesion among participants has been established. The sequence you choose depends on the purpose of your meeting. If the objective is straightforward and you expect little controversy in the meeting, you could safely start with the most important item.

If during your talks with participants before the meeting, you realize that group cohesion is required in order to deal with controversial agenda items, you should consider slotting them later in the meeting after you've established rapport within the group. Especially when you're dealing with potential controversy, concentrate on fewer, important agenda items, rather than having an exhausting number of items to consider.

As a way of adding interest in the agenda, solicit items for discussion from participants and give them recognition for their ideas. If you have guest speakers, allow them to contribute early in the meeting, so that they can leave and you can have privacy during the rest of the meeting. You also should decide whether you want to spend meeting time on items that are not on the agenda—something a participant brings up during the meeting. Nothing disrupts the purpose of a meeting more than discussing side issues and jumping between the items on the agenda. When people attend a meeting expecting to deal with one issue and the discussion doesn't meet this expectation, they might feel that they've wasted their time—and you have to have another meeting. Hopefully, your talks with participants prior to the meeting will jog their memories sufficiently to mention the addition prior to the start.

Agenda Item Process

After the agenda items are set up, establish a process or method for tackling each item. For example, will you have a whole-group discussion for an item, or will you break into small groups? In introducing the agenda, will you make a presentation with an overhead transparency or will you show a video clip of something? The process column tells how the agenda item will get done. Ideas for processes: group discussion, brainstorming session, presentation, interactive lecture, vote. If you're splitting a large group into smaller ones, indicate how this should work.

Following this, establish the amount of time you plan to spend on each agenda item. When time is crucial, this column becomes all-important. The "Responsible" column tells who is doing what in your meeting. Remember to contact these persons prior to your meeting, so that their participation will not be a surprise to them. The logistics area of the agenda can be an important time saver. The "preparation required" item tells participants what to read or gather or think about *before* they arrive at your meeting. Send handouts to everyone along with your agenda so they can come prepared to discuss and vote.

Structuring a Topic

Preparing and presenting are done in a different order.

Preparing	Presenting	
Write objective	Intro:	Opener
Select key points		Your introduction
Add supporting material		Meeting objective
Write transition statements		(Alternate spot for
Write preview and summary		your introduction)
Design the opening		Preview
Design the closing	Body:	Three key points
		Supporting material
		Two transitions
	Closing:	Summary
		To-do statement

Don't wait until the last minute to start preparing for public speaking. Develop your selected topic in stages and allot enough preparation time for plenty of practice before you speak. This is the best antidote for a bad case of nerves prior to speaking.

Preparation Order

1. Write the objective. What are you trying to get people to do? What do you want to accomplish by delivering this presentation? That's your objective—the object of presenting. Don't confuse your main points with your objective. An objective is a concise statement, usually one sentence, that conveys the main idea of your presentation. The objective is the first element you prepare because all of the rest of your presentation is designed to support it.

   Speakers can be dynamic and have interesting visuals; but if the audience can't remember the intent of the message or what they're supposed to do as a result of listening to the message, the presentation probably lacked a clearly defined objective. A presentation is usually aimed at getting people to understand something, or actually to do something. Don't forget to tell your audience what your objective is, either before or after introducing yourself.

2. Select the key points. The simpler and clearer your points, the easier it will be for your audience to remember your message. If you can, use the "rule of three" with your material. Most messages are organized into three main points, presumably based on what the audience can remember without losing interest.

Thinking through all your material and distilling the main points provides structure for grouping information. When you group information, the audience can understand it better.

Organizational schemes you can use:

- *Chronological order.* Key points can be presented in the order that they occur in time. Examples include what happened first, then what, then what; OR past, present, and future; OR first, second, and third steps.

- *Spatial arrangement.* Key points can be related by geographic areas—East, West, Midwest, South; or topographically—mountains, low-lying areas, deserts.

- *Topical approach.* Key points can be presented in the order of their importance. Take your listeners from the least significant point to more important ones, and then to the most important one.

For greater effect relate the point you want them to remember—the most important one—last.

- *Concerns/solutions.* Key points are presented in two categories. Examples include: problem/solution, advantages/disadvantages, objections/answers, ideal/reality, old way/new way, feature/benefits, and compare/contrast. Use this form when you have six or eight items you want to include and they logically fall into two categories.

Mnemonic devices help people remember your key points. Try using the first letter of each key word to form an acronym that people will remember (w w w). Or try phrasing your key points so that they all start with the same letter (push, pull, protect). Or form a word with your starting letters (M E M O).

3. Add supporting material for each key point. What will help people accept your major points? Key points alone are not sufficient to persuade people. You must include supporting materials that relate to the key point and create meaning for your audience, which, in turn, helps them remember your message.

Where does supporting material come from? Internal sources include information within the organization, such as newsletters or reports. Interviews can also yield useful material. If your presentation concerns improving a parking situation or the cafeteria, interviewing the parking services coordinator or the cafeteria manager should work. Two other sources for supporting material are external and personal. External sources are newspaper articles, books, trade journals, television shows, or the Internet. Personal sources come from your experience.

Supporting material may occur in one of these forms.

- *Examples.* Supplying a "for instance" or "for example" applies a general point to a specific person or event, making you more credible. Using a "word picture" of what could occur is also effective; with visualizing, the audience can better understand your key point.

- *Comparisons.* Clarifying a point by comparing it to something with which the audience is familiar helps them understand and makes them more receptive to your ideas. When a direct comparison isn't handy, use an analogy. An analogy implies that if two things are alike in one respect, they may be alike in other respects, too. Finally, using contrast shows points that oppose each other; differences are highlighted.

- *Quotations.* Providing a statement from a celebrity or an authority lends credence to key points. Make sure the "expert" is well known. Make sure you give credit to the author of the quote!

- *References, facts, numbers.* Supplying quantitative evidence from reports or statistics validates key points. Use only current data; make sure it's accurate.

Which of these types of supporting material should you use? All of them, in a balanced way. *Don't use one type of material to support all points.* How much supporting material should you use? Don't cover up the importance of your main points, but use enough to appear credible and convincing. Gather lots of information and have it ready. If you don't use it in the first meeting, you can use it in later meetings. Better to have too much than too little! Remember, you're distilling information for use.

Providing graphic support gives your audience a better idea of your key points.

- If you just show a picture and say nothing, comprehension and retention is **three and one-half** times greater than using words alone.

- Showing a picture *and* saying the words increase retention and comprehension to **six times** greater than words alone.

- Video clips are good; just don't treat everyone to a five-minute clip in a short meeting; one minute or less is fine.

4. Include transition statements between your major points. Transitions step listeners from one key point to the next. They are small but *critical* steps. Transitions help your listeners follow your thinking and make your message easier to remember. As a presenter, *you* know when you're moving on, but your audience doesn't, unless you use transitions.

Examples of transition statements are:

"After these two points, you'll be surprised by my third one."

"Now that we've considered the plus side, let's look at the minuses."

"First we looked at X, then we considered Y; now we're going to consider the most important of all—Z."

Pause in your delivery of transitional statements. *Don't rush through these!* Transitions add drama to your talk and make you appear a polished speaker, so make these count. One way to help the audience realize that you are going on to another point is to ask for questions after each key point. "Before we go on to my next point, I'd like to ask for questions. Anything need clarifying at this time?"

5. State your key points into brief sentence form, so that people are reminded of the highlights of your message. The audience is more likely to be persuaded by what they hear *frequently* and *recently*. The preview is a window that gives the audience an advance view of the key points. The summary reminds people of where they've been.

Format for a good presentation

Tell them what you're going to to tell them.
Tell them.
Tell them what you told them.

6. Design the opening. Figure out a way to get attention, pique curiosity, introduce your topic. What gets people's attention?

    • *Authoritative quotes* from a recognized authority. Celebrities, politicians, authors, and leaders are good to use. State your source's authority and what this expert does. Relate the quote to your topic.

    • *Rhetorical questions* invite attention because they involve the audience immediately. When you pose a question, people start mentally forming their replies, especially if it appeals to their curiosity.

    • *Declarative statements* make an attention-getting statement of fact. To get attention, address an issue of interest to the audience and deliver it expressively. A declarative statement stated without facial expression (deadpan) or the right tone of voice has little impact on your listeners.

    • *A scenario* makes up a scene that will grab your audience's attention. This technique makes a "word picture" that creates scenes in the minds of the audience. Use a real event or an imagined one. Maybe ask people to close their eyes; then wake them with a bang!

    • *An anecdote* describes an incident that's interesting, amusing, or biographical (or all three). Use facial expressions, gestures, and intonations to add interest and to bring your audience into your presentation. Audiences respond more when presenters relate on a human level, so showing an incident from your life improves rapport.

Introduce yourself somewhere *after* the opener and *before* you start listing your key points. Be brief and to the point. Don't linger on the introduction, but give enough information that the audience knows why you chose your topic. For example:

(*Opener*) "Have you ever gone up in a hot air balloon? I have and I'm here to tell you it's fun!"

(*Introduction*) "Hi! My name is _____."

(*Your background*) "Although I've only been up in the air once, I'm an instant fan of this sport."

(*Objective*) "Perhaps after my talk today, I can persuade some of you to try this amazing sport."

Do not think saying hello and your name is an opener! An opener has razzle-dazzle to it; it perks up the audience because you've aroused their curiosity. Your credentials or background reveal your expertise in the topic. How do you know what you know? Put this in your intro.

7. Design the closing. Ask the audience for agreement or action. Leave people something to do, and make this part of your close. State it in one of three ways: a reminder, an application of the information, or request for approval. "I encourage you to consider hot air ballooning as the exciting adventure I find it to be. Join me next Saturday!"

Presentation Order

Intro: Opener, your introduction, objective, (your introduction), preview
Body: Key points with supporting material; 2 transitions
Closing: Summary, to-do statement

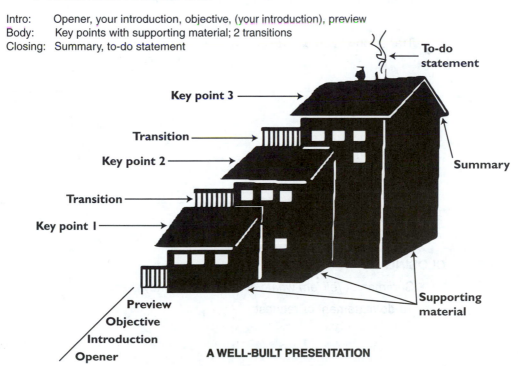

A WELL-BUILT PRESENTATION

If you can change the way people think, they will change the way they behave. Remember, however, that information alone doesn't persuade people. Strong presentation skills do!

PRACTICE EXERCISES FOR ORGANIZING MESSAGES

Directions: The next pages feature a format guide for organizing messages, a sample to show appropriate level of detail, and a practice exercise.

Format guide

MEETING OBJECTIVE: (*fill in this blank*)

INTRODUCTION

Opener: (*How will you get their attention?*)

Preview of talk: (*Tell 'em what you're going to tell 'em; the key points*)

BODY (*Tell 'em*)

Key Point 1 _____

Supporting facts/information/types of material:

Transition statement: (*actual words*)

Key Point 2 _____

Supporting material:

Transition statement:

Key Point 3 _____

Supporting material:

CLOSING

Summary: (*Tell 'em what you told 'em; the key points*)

To-do statement or request:

SAMPLE—ORGANIZING YOUR MESSAGE

Meeting Objective: *To inform about ways to help endangered species*

INTRO

Opener: *Endangered species inhabit only 7% of United States land area.*
(Show overhead of lovable endangered animal.)

Preview of talk: *I'm going to talk about several endangered species, what the government is doing to decrease these numbers, and organizations that aid the rescue of these ever-decreasing species.*

BODY

<u>Key Point 1</u>   *Number of endangered species*

Supporting material: *World Conservation Union's Red List*

Transition statement: *Although the numbers of species is extraordinary, our U.S. government is decreasing the numbers.*

<u>Key Point 2</u>   *1973 Endangered Species Act*

Supporting material: *Government document and magazine articles*

Transition statement: *Despite government action, other organizations support and devote funds to endangered animals.*

<u>Key Point 3</u>   *Organizations supporting endangered species*

Supporting material: *World Wildlife Federation and Internet organizations*

CLOSING

Summary: *I have talked about endangered species, what the U.S. government is doing to decrease the numbers of species, and what organizations are doing to help endangered species.*

To-do statement: *Think of ways to increase the numbers of endangered species in the U.S.*

Practice Exercise

This is a safety article from an insurance company. State a meeting objective and divide the information into three key points. Then add the remaining items.

preventing CAR JACKINGS & AUTO THEFT

- Be alert at stoplights and signs. One thief robs the motorist when he or she gets out to inspect the damage; the other thief steals the car.
- Don't apply make-up, shave, or read at stoplights. Don't be in a hurry to get to stoplights or signs—keep you car in motion if possible.
- Call ahead for safe directions. Lost or confused drivers are vulnerable.
- Don't drive near the curb in high-crime areas.
- Keep your doors locked and your windows shut when you drive.
- Keep your briefcase, purse, and packages under seats, or on the floor out of sight.
- Check your rearview mirror to make sure you are not followed into your driveway or garage.

If Approached by Strangers . . .

- When you park in an attended lot, leave only the ignition key.
- Drive off, if possible.
- Lean on your horn to attract attention.
- Leave everything behind if forced from your car.

When Parking Your Car . . .

- Lock your car when you go into a service station to pay for gas.
- Park in well-lighted, populated areas.
- Don't park next to a dumpster or anywhere thieves can hide.
- When possible, park on the ground level in garages so you avoid elevators and stairwells.

- Lock your car whenever you park it—4 out of 5 cars stolen are left unlocked.
- When returning to your vehicle, have your key ready. If anyone is hanging around your car, go back inside and ask for an escort.

PRACTICE EXERCISE

MEETING OBJECTIVE: (*fill in this blank*)

INTRODUCTION

 Opener: (*How will you get their attention?*)

 Preview of talk: (*Tell 'em what you're going to tell 'em; the key points*)

BODY (*Tell 'em*)

 Key Point 1 _____

 Supporting facts/information/types of material:

 Transition statement: (*actual words*)

 Key Point 2 _____

 Supporting material:

 Transition statement:

 Key Point 3 _____

 Supporting material:

CLOSING

 Summary: (*Tell 'em what you told 'em; the key points*)

 To-do statement or request:

3
Conducting Information Meetings

Where do we line up for the charisma shots? There must be an injection or a pill we can take that will transform us into warm, inviting, relaxed persons whose preparation and polish cause the audience to listen raptly and react enthusiastically to our to-do statements. They leave our meetings filled with purpose, always willing to attend our future meetings because we lead so well. Ah, were it so! Although pharmaceuticals are being introduced rapidly these days, meeting management cure-alls don't come in quick-fix modes. Instead, we have algorithms that produce the same effect. These procedures for accomplishing the end result—effective meeting management—just take longer to develop. Their advantage over drugs and shots is that once you see what it takes, you improve naturally!

DUMB THINGS MEETING LEADERS DO

Poor first impression
Dull, dry, boring
Frozen in one spot
Poor facial expression
Weak eye contact
No audience involvement
No enthusiasm
Inaudible voice
Poor visual aids
Inept use of visual aids

Platform Conduct

When you first step before a group, you are an unknown quantity for 120 seconds. (Peoples, 1992.) The old saying, "You never get a second chance to make a first impression" is true. In two minutes, people make assessments about you that will determine whether they will listen and ultimately follow your lead. Surprising as it may seem, people pay more assessment attention to the visual and vocal cues they see and hear than your actual words. Dr. Albert Mehrabian studied face-to-face communication looking for the channels of communication delivery people heed in assessing speakers. His findings are shown in this chart.

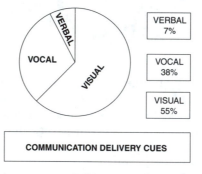

COMMUNICATION DELIVERY CUES

Appearance counts!   Voice counts!   Words count!

Charismatic people are skilled in the verbal side of communication, but they're also good at nonverbal communication. Part of charisma is "presence." It's your bearing, your carriage, your poise which helps you create a bond with your audience. How do you establish "presence?" A major part of presence is emotional expressivity, which can be verbal or nonverbal. Leaders can "infect" followers, stir them to action, through facial expressions, body movements, and posture, as well as words.

Most of us enjoy being emotionally aroused because it makes us feel alive. We seek emotionally arousing entertainment and, although entertainment is a temporary "fix," we use it sometimes with the hope of making more permanent changes in our emotional outlooks. We enjoy motivational speakers because of the positive emotions they convey. Through their emotional expressiveness, they spark an emotional reaction in listeners.

As listeners, we are also affected by the subtle emotional cues given off by those who surround us. A chain reaction can occur, so that the audience becomes emotionally charged. Emotional expressivity enables speakers to arouse feelings in an audience by establishing emotional ties to the audience. We want to feel that our leader likes us, cares for us and our feelings, and is concerned for us. When we feel that a leader meets us where we are and understands our concerns, we more readily accept their reassurance and comfort. We are more willing to listen—and follow. So, how do we as meeting leaders convey this?

Appearance

One of the first aspects of appearance most folks think of is clothing and its accessories, so let's look at that first. The guideline here is to contribute to the perception you want to create. If it's businesslike, bring out your suit and dress shoes. If it's less formal, note acceptable standards for casual clothes and wear those. Our current culture may consider "dressing up" an unnecessary concern. However, when you pay attention to clothing, you're saying "I care enough about your perception of me to dress appropriately." Some studies indicate that when you're dressed in your best bib and tucker, you perform better because you feel good about yourself.

A second guideline is that your clothing and accessories should not detract from your message. We've all noticed a speaker with HUGE earrings, or fluttering fabrics, or a necktie that speaks louder than the message itself. Although we're in the age of wash-and-wear clothing, we still need an iron now and then. A word about buttoning your jacket: do it. Some style analysts have said that an unbuttoned suit jacket makes you look approachable. Buttoned looks better. Convey approachability by your nonverbal behavior, not your clothing, especially if you're wearing a double-breasted jacket (one with a double row of buttons in the front). Try to look the part you want to play.

Nonverbal Behavior

What you *do* speaks louder that what you say. Remember the Mehrabian percentages: **visual is 55 percent, verbal is 38 percent, and words are 7 percent.** At this point, let's say that you have the proper dress angle figured out. Now what? What else goes into the visual picture you are trying to create?

Good posture conveys presence. Straight shoulders and back look like you mean business, but don't go overboard here. Standing "at attention" while speaking may not work well either. Strike a balance. Try to move confidently and purposefully. If you've planned your meeting well, you should know exactly what you need to do prior to the meeting and what your goals are during the meeting, so this lends credence to your movements. Don't stand in one place; walk out into your audience occasionally. If you wish to plan this, make one point standing in one spot, the second in another, and the third in another. If you're using overheads and need to stay near the projector, leave one on for a while, step out in front of the projector, and deliver your supporting material from there. Don't pace or sway from side to side just to create movement. People get dizzy if you pace back and forth during meetings.

The final set of appearance indicators center on your head, face, and eyes. **Of these, most important are your eyes.** Obviously, if your head is buried in your notes, eye contact with the audience is limited, so practice enough that you can do major parts of your talk without notes. Use note cards preferably. If you must use sheets of paper, glance at them only briefly and maintain eye contact. Don't look at the ceiling or the floor or above the heads of the crowd or just at the people who nod their heads and smile at you. Look at one person in the audience for about five seconds or until you've finished the phrase or sentence or thought, and move on to another person, maybe across the room. Then choose someone else. (Saying their names while you're doing this is especially riveting.) You're creating a series of one-on-one conversations in doing this, which makes people feel you understand them and have their best interests at heart.

Keep the room lights as bright as possible so folks can see your face. You are your own best audiovisual. *You are the show!* Smile at the audience, act alert, attentive, and confident and your audience will respond similarly. If you hesitate or act unsure, your audience will think, "If you are not certain about this, why should we be?" Plus your uneasiness is catching; soon your audience feels restless and out of sorts. It's the expressivity thing!

Voice

Body language and voice express your feelings, attitudes, physical state, and self-image. Good vocal quality energizes people and adds meaning to your words. A clear, pleasing, expressive voice with good articulation communicates your ideas well and keeps the audience's attention. People will remember what you say and be more willing to respond to you.

What does your voice sound like to others? Tape record yourself—audio or video—and listen critically to your speech patterns, your energy level, your listenability. It's said that we acquire our voices by hearing and imitating our families in growing up. However, we're not stuck with what we inherited or learned early on. Work on improving your vocal instrument!

The first rule of the voice is to be heard. Even if you're the shy, retiring type who ducks his/her head and almost whispers responses to others, you must be heard in order to lead meetings. Some people are soft-spoken by nature; they just don't jump up and down a lot in public. Yet at sporting events or while pursuing a hobby or topic near their hearts, they have enough volume and intensity for two persons. Harness this sound production unit for meetings! This isn't a voice problem; it's a self-image problem and, maybe, a breath control problem.

Contrary to what most people think, your voice doesn't originate in your throat. It starts in your diaphragm, a dome-shaped muscle underneath your lungs and above your stomach. The diaphragm flattens out when we inhale and our lungs take in air. Sound is actually produced when we exhale. Air from our lungs comes through the trachea and causes the larynx to vibrate. The amount of resonance in our voices, that pleasant "hum" that makes some people easy to listen to, is determined by the chest, throat, and nasal passages. Sounds are determined by our jawbones, noses, tongues, and mouth parts. If we experience muscle tension in any of this network, we produce different sounds. A shrill or harsh voice, a too-low or too-high pitch, or a choppy speech pattern can be attributed to breath control problems. (D'Arcy, 1992.)

You can determine the amount of diaphragmatic breathing you use by holding your hands over your stomach above the waist and panting. In speaking, we must push air from the diaphragm *through* the vocal cords to the nose and mouth areas. If you have an itsy-bitsy voice and people are constantly asking you to repeat what you just said, work with your breathing. Since the diaphragm is a muscle, you can exercise it and train your voice to produce more sound.

If you have a big voice to start with, be aware that steady volume wears on people, so you need to vary this quality. Have you ever worked with a person who used the same volume level all the time whether he was two feet away or across the room? Continually loud voices hurt others' ears. Projecting your voice so it reaches all of the audience is important, too. Some speakers address only the front rows of a crowd, while the people in the back steadily lose interest. Share your message with the entire group!

Voice characteristics you can work on besides volume include rate, pitch, and articulation. Rate is how quickly or slowly you speak. People can listen at a much higher rate than most people can speak. An average rate of speech is 140 words per minute. However, if you're making a technical presentation, you could slow down to 100 words per minute. Then speed up on other points, since a consistently slow rate of speech makes you sound tired or bored. *Pauses create drama and emphasis.* (Arredondo, 1994.)

Pitch concerns the low and the high of your sound and is one of the best qualities to improve your expressivity. Young people tend to have higher-pitched voices so we associate high pitch with immaturity. A really high-pitch sounds shrill and lacks strength. Try for a lower pitch; it is much more pleasant to hear and your voice carries farther. Use pitch changes to show a change in your message. End declarative sentences with a drop in pitch to emphasize the authority of your statement. Lift your pitch at the end of questions since this indicates uncertainty. Vary your pitch with your meaning; otherwise, you sound artificial.

Inflection is the variation of tone in your voice. We would get bored listening to one note on a piano or even three notes, for that matter. Vary your inflection and pitch to maintain listener interest. A monotone speaker or even a three-note speaker sounds flat and lifeless. A hesitant tone sounds timid and indecisive, while a harsh tone sounds aggressive. A nasal tone lacks authority. All these aspects can be improved, but you must listen to yourself and get feedback from others in order to correct them. If you are happy and enthusiastic or stressed and tired, it will show in your tone of voice. Smile in your head and it will come out through your voice.

Articulation is the distinctness of your words. Vernacular errors, such as jest for just, fer for far, orl for oil, warsh for wash, make people think you are uneducated. Better to eliminate dialect pronunciations in favor of more cultured language. An offshoot of this is not pronouncing the endings of words, such as comin' and goin' or wanna. These make you sound lazy; use your lips and tongue to create words and be sure to finish them.

A last word on voice is the use of fillers: um, ah, you know, like. Use *pauses* rather than fill in with meaningless words.

Visuals

Nothing adds to your professionalism more than handling visuals well. This means you should practice with them, so that you're comfortable using them. Let's consider which visuals make the best impression

Real things beat everything else. A 30-second demonstration, several cans of food supplements, a vegetarian pizza, a set of golf clubs—depending on your topic,

VOCAL PRESENTATION STYLE CHECKLIST

SPEAKER'S NAME:

RATE

1. Could be slower _____   Could be faster _____   Good rate _____
2. Needs smoothing; choppy phrasing _____

    Phrasing OK; work on variety _____

VOLUME

1. Too soft _____   Too loud _____   Volume fine _____
2. Same volume throughout _____   Good variety _____

PITCH

1. Level could be lower _____   Level could be higher _____

    Level OK __
2. Repetitive pitch pattern _____   Good variety _____

INFLECTION

1. Harsh sound _____   Timid sound _____   Tone OK _____
2. Flat sound _____   Rich, resonant sound _____

ARTICULATION

1. Emphasize consonants more _____   Good, distinct words _____
2. Word endings omitted _____   Clear word delivery _____
3. Lips hardly moved _____   Good lip movement _____

Comments:

of course—will create enthusiasm in the crowd. If you are representing a company or a department in that company, wearing indigenous work garb characterizes ideas well. Other possibilities: models of real things and pictures of real things using videotapes, photos, display boards, overhead transparencies, and so on.

Overheads are used extensively in many areas. Here are some tips for using them more professionally.

1. Use 18 point fonts (sans serif) at minimum on overheads. Use no more than 5-6 lines of print per overhead. Don't go berserk with graphics.

2. Either have an overhead on or turn the projector off. No white screens while you're standing off to the side talking and no white screens between transparencies. Put something on!

3. Leave overheads on long enough for the audience to read them. Don't use a transparency if you don't have time to talk about it.

4. Lay a pen or pencil on the overhead plate as a pointer for a discussion item. DON'T USE YOUR FINGERS. Use a red light pointer only if you can hold it very steady, which most folks can't. Don't beat the projection screen to pieces either with a pointer or your hands.

5. Take time to check the visual fit of your overheads before you start talking. Make sure each is level for the reader and that the light from the projector is square with and on the screen.

6. Put information on the top third of the transparency. Push the images to the top of the screen as you talk. Use a sheet of paper to cover future discussion items and reveal the image as you talk about it.

7. Practice with your overheads at least five times before you present. Time yourself; videotape yourself, if possible. Plan segments you can leave out if time is short. Many people spend far too much time on the first few points and have to rush through the last point, which usually is the most important part of the presentation.

8. If you have lots of information the audience needs to have, make handouts for them, and create overheads with ONLY key words and concepts. *DO NOT make an overhead of an agenda that you hand out. DO NOT make overheads of single, typewritten sheets of information.* People can't read these and then they start to get irritated!

9. To create good overheads, look at the content of your talk, decide what the main ideas are, and make overheads from your analysis. Use pictures, cartoons, photos; leave a word picture of your talk. People will forget 75 percent of what you *say* within 24 hours, UNLESS you show them a picture and repeat what you want them to remember. Then they're *six* times more likely to remember what you said.

10. Talk your talk. Don't read it or recite it. Don't read overhead content word for word to the audience. (They, too, can read.) Don't turn your back to the audience in order to read material on the screen. Look at your info on the projection plate itself; maintain eye contact.

If you're using overheads, it looks polished to create an opening transparency you can leave on while you're setting up for the talk. To determine whether a visual of any sort is large enough for folks in the back to see, put it on the floor and stand up; if you can read it from there, it's OK. If you have several transparencies you intend to use, decide where you'll draw and discard. Put them on the left of the projector and discard on the right or whatever. Don't use audience time to file your overheads into a three-ring notebook. The audience gets more caught up in your filing than your topic. Leave the room lights on as much as possible when using visuals.

REMINDERS

Only use key words, phrases, diagrams
Make material easy to understand
Use no more than 5-6 lines of writing
Use no more than 6-7 words in each line
Use upper third of the transparency

Check the focus before you start
Check each transparency—level and on screen
Look at the audience; don't look at the screen
Use a pen or pencil as a pointer on the transparency

Turn off the projector when talk varies from transparency
Keep projector on when using several overheads
Put new one on as you remove the old
Use the revelation technique to mask information

Preparation

Now for a series of quick tips on presenting:

- Don't apologize for anything once you rise to your feet. Don't say you're sorry about your overheads, your preparation for the meeting, your manner of dress, the length of the meeting—nothing. Apologizing just makes people think you didn't care enough to correct whatever is wrong. We're trying to convince people we *do* care. It's the presence thing!

- Don't tell jokes. For some reason people think these are good openers, but they aren't, especially if they're corny or make fun of a race, a profession, or a status. Better to tell a personal story which pokes fun at you; humor is an event far enough in your past to be considered funny.

- Don't start a presentation with an organization chart or a dictionary definition of a word. For example, expressivity means vivid depiction of a mood or sentiment. Isn't this riveting! (Yawn)

- Don't tell the audience more than they want to know. Your job as a presenter is to distill the information you have into appropriately sized chunks, including enough specifics to get the meaning across but not explaining every jot and tittle of the subject at hand.

- Good content alone can't save a badly delivered presentation. You can have good material, well-constructed overheads—the works! But if you can't deliver your message well, folks won't listen or do what you want.

- Don't try to "wing" presentations or meetings. Prepare and practice. Create a written script which includes everything you want to do. Then write key thoughts on notecards to use during your talk or meeting.

- Keep your hands away from your nose, your glasses, your hair, your tie, your jewelry, your pocket change, whatever. Constant fiddling with these makes you appear nervous and that makes the audience uncomfortable. Then they stop listening altogether and start counting the number of times you do this. Same thing with ums, ahs, you know, and like.

- Use your hands and arms for gesturing to emphasize your point, but don't raise your arms up and put them down methodically because it's good to use gestures. Inexperienced performers on stage provide examples of this. Practice using appropriate gestures.

- If you find yourself wringing your hands while speaking or clapping your hands inadvertently but often, work on holding them in front of you at waist level calmly clasped, much as a trained singer does at times.

- Putting your hands in your pockets occasionally is OK. Just don't jam them in there permanently. Don't play with your pocket knife or money you may have stashed there.

- Don't point your index finger at people. In some cultures finger pointing is a big no-no; in presenting it's just considered rude. Keep your fingers together and extend your hand palm up to call on someone.

- Answer the question, What's in it for me. Why should the people sitting in your meeting be there? People want to gain in some way in return for the time they give you—money, control, opportunity, enjoyment, time, popularity. Everyone tunes into Station WIIFM (what's in it for me).

- People enjoy uniqueness and variety, so plan for that. Most people speak 120 to 200 words per minute, but can hear 600 words per minute. Their minds wander if you don't refocus their attention through a visual, a question, an unexpected action—something to bring them back. Remember that people will forget 75 percent of what you say within 24 hours. If you show a picture and say your words, retention is six times greater. We keep 10 percent of what we read, 20 percent of what we hear, 30 percent of what we see, and 50 percent of what we see and hear (Peoples, 1992).

Finally, good leaders are responsive to followers' needs and show successes or gains for groups. Make meetings count—with gains for all involved.

OK, we're ready! Time to present the information meeting! You've selected your topic, gathered LOTS of supporting material on the key points, have the closing and opening planned. Check your wardrobe for appropriate togs: women are wearing dresses, suits, pants suits, dressy blouses, and skirts; men are wearing suits, dress slacks, and IRONED shirts with ties. Wear formal business clothes as though you were going to an important interview. Exceptions: if you're representing a faction of some sort, you may dress in indigenous garb. Examples: McDonalds manager, fire-fighter, emergency medical technician, marathon runner, golfer (knickers are nice); any occupation in which a recognized uniform is worn.

Included here are:

- an Agenda Form: copy enough for each meeting member
- the Information Meeting Critique: grading items and points
- an Observation Sheet: each person will be asked to critique one other person after his/her meeting. Just watch the speaker and fill out the sheet. When the person ends the presentation, get the microphone from them, and comment on the performance. Remember to limit negatives to two items and list strong points especially.
- a Self-Critique: watch your video after your meeting and write your answers to the questions asked

AGENDA FOR INFORMATION MEETING

Meeting Objective:

Logistics	*Meeting Members*
Date:	1. Leader:
Time:	2. Attendees:
Location:	Meeting called by:
	Phone:

Agenda Item	Process	Time	Who's Responsible

INFORMATION MEETING CRITIQUE

LEADER: **OBSERVER:**   **PTS. POSSIBLE: 30**

PREPARATION:

    Professional appearance (interview quality)   (3) _____

    Good quality & quantity visual aids   (3) _____

    Well written agenda   (1) _____

PRESENTATION:

INTRODUCTION: Opener; creating interest   (2) _____

                  Objective well specified   (1) _____

                  Your intro/credentials   (1) _____

                  Preview of talk   (2) _____

BODY: Three key points   (3) _____

                     Chronological ____   Spatial ____

                     Order of importance (topical) ____

                     Concerns/solutions ____

                  Supporting material for each   (3) _____

                     References____   Examples____

                     Analogies____   Quotes____

                     Facts____   Numbers____

                  Transitions from point to point   (2) _____

CLOSING: Summary   (2) _____

                  Ask for agreement or action   (1) _____

PERFORMANCE:

                  Time management (10 minutes)   (2) _____

                  Eye contact with audience   (1) _____

                  Voice: (1) _____
                    Rate____   Volume____

                  Enthusiasm   (2) _____

                  TOTAL POINTS EARNED

Comments:

OBSERVATION SHEET for Information Meeting

PRESENTER: OBSERVER:

5—Excellent	4—Good	3—Average	2—Needs work	1—Poor

PERSONAL PREPARATION

	5	4	3	2	1
1. Appropriate business attire	5	4	3	2	1
2. Voice quality/tone	5	4	3	2	1
3. Voice audibility	5	4	3	2	1
4. Confidence displayed	5	4	3	2	1

PRESENTATION PREPARATION

	5	4	3	2	1
5. Good organization	5	4	3	2	1
6. Meaningful topic/key point development	5	4	3	2	1
7. Attention-getting opening/closing	5	4	3	2	1
8. Easy-to-follow delivery	5	4	3	2	1
9. Rehearsed performance	5	4	3	2	1

PROJECTION

	5	4	3	2	1
10. Vocal effectiveness (intonation, fillers, pauses)	5	4	3	2	1
11. Audience interaction/eye contact	5	4	3	2	1
12. Energy/enthusiasm portrayed	5	4	3	2	1

STRONG POINTS: WORK ON:

INFORMATION MEETING SELF-CRITIQUE/SINGLE CONFERENCE REPORT

Name: Meeting Time:

Stated Objective of Talk:

A. PREPARATION:

    Did you appear professional?

    Were your visuals readable?

    Was your topic a good choice for you?

B. PRESENTATION:

    Opening: What was your opener and was it effective?

                Did you tell us what your qualifications were?

    Body:

                Where did you get your supporting material?

                Were your transitions clearly stated?

    Closing:

                Did you go over your main points?

                What was effective about your close?

C. PERFORMANCE:

                How well did you "fill the room with your presence?"

                Did you portray enthusiasm?

                Comment on your voice:

List two things you think you did well:

List two things you want to work on:

4

Preparing for Interactive Meetings

Have you attended a meeting and walked away afterward thinking "THAT was a waste of time!" or, "Why didn't we get anything done?" In our time-oriented culture, wasting time (and money) in meetings is serious. This next section will teach you how to prepare for meetings and how to conduct them so that meeting objectives are accomplished, participants feel their views have been considered, and good decisions have been made.

Why Have Meetings?

A majority of groups and organizations couldn't function without meetings. *Interacting face to face with other people is the best way to communicate when what YOU say depends on what OTHER PEOPLE say.* You can react immediately to others' ideas; you can come up with new alternatives and problem solutions; you can discuss the repercussions of actions a group or organization is considering—all of which you can't do sitting alone at your desk. Of course, there's electronic mail at your desk, which eases the process of communication, but email lacks the visual and vocal elements of communication necessary for perception of meaning.

A group meeting together becomes more than the sum of its parts. Groups are comprised of people with knowledge and experiences that vary—they bring different resources to discussions. Especially in today's culture, problems extend beyond the boundaries of set disciplines or knowledge bases, so it is becoming increasingly important that people with varying backgrounds and viewpoints be brought together to discuss and decide.

An additional impetus for having meetings is that of implementing decisions. When people have the chance to present "their side" of an issue and when they can participate in making decisions on the issue, they are far more ready to implement a group decision, even though the decision may not be what they originally wanted. Sharing information, creating alternatives, and considering the potential aftermath of decisions are powerful ways to change people's minds and motivate them to change behavior. Learning to lead this process is essential for managers.

Part of the need for meetings concerns psychological needs of people. We need to feel we are part of an organization or a member of a team. We also need a sense of togetherness, belonging, and trust, we need help with responsibilities, and we need a renewed sense of commitment to our work groups and the organization. Meetings foster these needs. They are intensive ways of involving others in solving problems and making decisions. When people meet together for long periods of time or deal intensively for shorter periods, they often feel a sense of comradery with other group members. The time spent sharing experiences, stating personal views, and cooperating with others to find the best solution for all concerned creates a feeling of connectedness, a sense of community. Groups of people meeting together are potentially powerful. Leading efficient and effective meetings is important for managers!

Interacting face to face with others is the BEST way to communicate when what YOU say depends on what other people say.

What's Wrong with Meetings?

So what's wrong with meetings? A lot of it has to do with the way they're conducted—the meeting process itself. When groups of people get together to discuss things, it helps if there is a standard conduct, a method for insuring that all factions represented are heard. A standard for meetings is *Robert's Rules of Order*. Written by General Henry M. Robert in 1876, these rules enforce parliamentary procedure, which came from the English Parliament at that time. Henry Robert was ordered to San Francisco in 1867 as part of the Army Engineers; he found a tumultuous place where various constituents had quite different ideas about how things got done.

Using the United States House of Representatives model, he developed a standard for meeting conduct, not to achieve consensus necessarily, but to insure "deliberation," or "working through" the issues. Inherent in deliberation is the right of the minority to be heard along with the majority, so that decisions are made by a majority of meeting constituents ONLY after considering the views of all persons potentially affected by them. The parliamentary model requires a chairperson who controls the discussion and a secretary who takes minutes, a record of what is discussed and decided. It also requires of participants an extensive knowledge of Robert's Rules.

That's part of what's wrong with meetings. In formal meetings today when Robert's Rules are used (and they still are), the chairperson must be adroit in Robertese, and participants need to be fairly skilled in the process. The Rules bring an accepted order to meetings, but some people view this as an encumbrance to expression. Another part of what's wrong is that this meeting process isn't suited to solving problems informally by collaborating, working together on complex issues that are interdependent. However, other protocols do not have universal acceptance.

A lack of standards for meetings makes conflict difficult to resolve, creates dilemmas when decisions are made without input from those affected by decisions, and makes leading a productive meeting difficult.

The meeting process you are about to learn shows the way to conduct efficient and effective meetings. You will learn how to prepare for and conduct meetings so that problem solving is done with spontaneity and decision making is direct and objective. Having learned these skills, you will be viewed as a leader with merit while being perceived as empathetic and humble. Your secret—knowing that process determines outcome. By controlling the meeting process, you CAN determine what will happen. Effective meetings produce sound decisions, and organizations run on decisions at all levels.

Secret to Success:

Knowing that meeting process determines outcome

Types of Meetings

Meetings in organizations usually have one of these purposes: information giving, information exchange, problem solving, and decision making.

Information-giving meetings are favored when:

- new programs or policies are announced or updated;
- clients need to be sold on company products or services;
- employees need training on new equipment or procedures;
- employees need to build up their team spirit.

Information-exchange meetings are called for when:

- the information is complex or controversial;
- the information has major implications for the meeting participants;
- there is symbolic value to a personal approach.

Again, memos work here, but phone calls are better, and, increasingly, electronic mail allows information exchange more quickly.

Problem-solving meetings allow several people to combine knowledge and skills at once. These are useful when:

- a problem requires immediate response;
- a staff considers operational difficulties in new products/processes;
- a conflict or difference of opinion is possible;
- people need to be persuaded to change their minds on an issue.

There aren't many good alternatives to face-to-face communication, but conference calls, interactive videos, and Web chat rooms are possible.

Decision-making meetings are needed:

- as follow-ups to problem-solving discussions;
- for majority decisions or evaluations on issues.

It may be possible to use telephone surveys or mailed response sheets for these, but the feeling of closure on an issue is more complete if done by face-to-face agreement.

THE IMPORTANT CONSIDERATION FOR MANAGERS IS: DO WE NEED TO HAVE A MEETING? A rule of thumb to use in determining whether to have a meeting is to ask if you are sure of the outcome. If you already know the answer, you could telephone, write, or not have a meeting. If you aren't sure how you OR the issue will be received AND this is important to you or your company, better to go in person and have a meeting.

If you know, don't go!

If you don't know, do it!

Meeting Approaches

Two general approaches to meetings are leader-controlled and group-centered. *Leader-controlled approaches* are used at information-giving meetings and large group meetings when the flow of open information is difficult. The leader opens the meeting, either makes announcements or calls on others to do so, and calls for questions and comments. In other words, the leader is the show. This approach is easy on the leader since there are few surprises, and large amounts of information can be covered in short periods of time. The disadvantages of this approach are that the free flow of information is stymied somewhat by having to go through the leader to get "air time," so spontaneity is affected. Another disadvantage is that sensitive or emotional issues usually don't emerge, and all the participants don't have a chance to be heard.

In *group-centered approaches*, the leader runs the show, but is not a dominant figure. Participants interact more freely and address questions to each other, while the leader keeps the meeting moving on, redirecting the focus of comments that stray from the meeting purpose, ensuring that all persons participate, and summarizing the apparent position of the group from time to time. This approach is more difficult for the leader, especially dealing with the increased interaction and the emotions sometimes generated. Advantages of this type of meeting are that people understand others' viewpoints better, more information generally leads to a better decision, and when people express themselves, they feel better. Disadvantages include the increased amount of time needed and the fact that having interpersonal discussions in large groups is difficult when meaningful exchange is important.

Which approach you use in meetings depends on you and your meeting objective—why you're holding the meeting.

Now, a word about you. Meetings should be quite important to you personally. No one sees you at your desk or in your office working on reports or telephoning or working at your computer. They see the results of these activities, which are necessary, but conducting meetings benefits your image in the company in different ways. Others see you in action in meetings and form opinions about your competence based on what they see and hear. If you can cut through chaos to find the issues that matter, get groups to deliberate these issues and lead decision making on these issues, you can become known as a competent leader in your organization. Preparing for and conducting meetings is essential to being a good leader.

When to Have Meetings

By now, we know some reasons *not* to have group meetings:

- You've already made up your mind or your boss has made up his/hers;
- The subject can be addressed by other means of communication (phone, memo, email, etc.).

Let's add to these by including:

- Lack of time to prepare for a meeting;
- Lack of data;
- A subject of a confidential nature which should not be shared with others in the work group. Issues like hiring, firing, negotiating salaries, and evaluating performance are better dealt with in one-on-one meetings.

Calling a meeting is GOOD when:

- You want information or advice from groups;
- You want group help in solving a problem or making a decision;
- An issue needs discussion for the way it impacts the organization;
- You want a meeting OR the group wants a meeting;

- A problem exists between groups;
- A problem exists, but the problem and who's responsible for dealing with it are not clear.

Key to your preparation for a meeting is the meeting objective. What is your purpose in having a meeting? What is the main goal of getting people together for your meeting? If your objective addresses one of the previously mentioned reasons for having a meeting, then you can start preparing in depth. A meeting objective should be brief, concise, and written as a clear goal, rather than a vague statement. Use action verbs with "to," such as to inform, to create, to decide.

Planning Interactive Meetings

A meeting leader may be a manager, a supervisor, an employee, or a number of other people; however, the responsibilities for planning meetings are the same. These are: preparing the agenda, considering logistics, selecting attendees, and calculating meeting costs. It may help simply to take a sheet of paper and write down what the meeting will be like: What kind of meeting you want, who should be invited, when it should be scheduled, where it will take place, what issues will surface, what decisions need to be made, what information you need to lead the meeting, what written materials will be needed, what audiovisual aids will work best—everything you can think of at this point.

CREATING AN AGENDA FOR EVERY MEETING IS THE MOST IMPORTANT STEP IN ENSURING SUCCESSFUL MEETINGS. Plus it's a natural offshoot of the page of notes you just wrote. Why use an agenda? *It draws a big picture of the meeting and serves to focus thoughts and discussion on the purpose of your meeting.* It also details the assignments for meeting participants and lets them know how to prepare for the meeting, since leaders circulate the agenda at least two days ahead of the actual meeting. At a glance, participants will know the purpose of the meeting, the time, location, what they should bring or do for the meeting, who will be there, and how the meeting will be conducted. You've already written the meeting objective as specifically as you can. The next step is to set up the when, where, what, and who of the meeting.

When

The choice of meeting time depends on the purpose of your meeting, the availability of key people and facilities, and how long you think the meeting will take. If you've planned a two-hour meeting, you wouldn't start it at 11:00, since lunchtime would interfere. Speaking of lunchtime, consider whether you want to combine a meeting with a meal. There are pros and cons on both sides of this issue. Having meals and meetings combined emphasizes sociability and networking, but may distract people from the purpose of the meeting, especially evening meals.

Sharing food is a way of building bonds between people, though. You might consider having special treats at group meetings—doughnuts or bagels in the morning, cookies or crackers and cheese in the afternoon. Coffee, tea, juice, and sodas are also welcome. Breakfast meetings work for some, since you catch people before they go to their jobs, and meetings tend to be short and productive.

It's best to avoid scheduling meetings on holidays, long weekends, or the beginning or end of the week. Morning meetings summon longer attention spans for some; as the day progresses and tasks mount up to distract people, their patience and willingness to contribute wears thin. Sales meetings might be held early in the morning to hand out assignments and point out daily or weekly goals. If you do schedule morning meetings, give employees a chance to get settled before gathering up for your meeting.

Line workers and staff connected with them usually have meetings before or after their shift hours. Employees who have contacts with customers will want to be free when customers are likely to call or visit. If no compensation is provided for job-related meetings, employees will probably resent returning in the evenings or on days off for meetings.

Where

Sometimes you have no choice; you have meetings in whatever size room will accommodate the number of participants you have. If people are seated for a long period of time, you should arrange for comfortable chairs. You should eliminate distractions such as phone calls, foot traffic, and interruptions in whatever form they arrive. A conference table is desirable for group discussions. Try for as much eye contact as possible between participants, whatever seating arrangements you have. Set up a circle or a horseshoe arrangement for maximum interaction. Moveable chairs also work for small break-out groups as well. Other seating arrangements are:

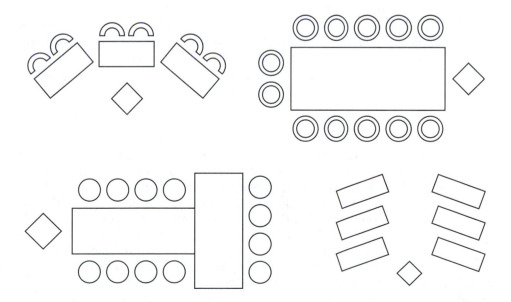

What

A major objective in meeting preparation is to gather as much information as you can and consider the implications of the information. Especially if the subject of your meeting is controversial as well as important, you should contact participants before the actual meeting. Anticipate what questions you think you'll get and find answers to those questions. The contacts you make will help you anticipate areas of agreement and disagreement during your actual meeting. As you talk with people, solicit their personal views on your topic. If they have "hidden agendas," you can be prepared to counteract their tactics. If enough data exists prior to the meeting, create handouts and send them to participants with a request to read them before the meeting. As we've already said, send out your agenda in advance to clarify the meeting purpose. Again, your agenda needs an objective, a notice of the time/date/location of the meeting, a list of attendees, and discussion items.

Who

The right number of people and the right people at your meeting are crucial elements in the success of meetings. More people attending means increased meeting costs, longer discussion times, and less opportunity for participation. If large groups are inevitable, try break-out groups to maximize participation. Limit your agenda items for large groups.

A good rule of thumb in selecting attendees is including those who can be directly helpful in carrying out the objective of the meeting. If you are making major decisions, include someone directly affected by the changes you are considering. Consider who has the power to make decisions and who will implement them. Select attendees who support your objective, who oppose it, and the undecided. Finally, consider people it is politically expedient to invite, those who might cause trouble if you didn't invite them, as well as those you're obliged to invite for any number of reasons. If you can, avoid inviting known meeting disrupters; no one needs long-winded people who disagree with everyone on all the issues. Consider also that some people will consider it a blessing not to be asked to attend. If they are not directly affected by the objective of the meeting, offer to send them a copy of the minutes as a courtesy.

Costs

If you succeed in establishing a more efficient method of conducting meetings, you will have saved time and money!

We've looked at preparing an agenda, considering logistics, and selecting attendees. A final consideration is figuring out the costs of the meeting. **If more people figured the actual costs of meeting, fewer of them might be held.** To figure time costs, write down the names of all attendees at your meeting and figure their time value. This could be hourly pay or a percentage of their total salary, divided by the number of days each year that they are required to work. Multiply the time value per hour by the length of your meeting to get the cost for each attendee. Then figure preparation time and costs, any handouts or visuals made, room costs, refreshments, transportation, and guest speaker costs. Add all this to find the total meeting cost.

Return on investment of time and money in a meeting depends on the value of the results produced. Well-planned, well-executed meetings should produce *better* results in *shorter* time frames and be more cost effective as a result. Figuring the monetary value of results may prove difficult unless you can directly connect a result with a figure from the "bottom line," such as:

- decreased operating expense
- hourly wages saved
- productivity improvement

Track savings in the beginning of your stint as a meeting leader and continue to monitor your efficiency and that of your work group. Then **DOCUMENT SAVINGS OF TIME AND MONEY—IT'S YOUR TICKET TO**

PAY, PRESTIGE, AND PROMOTION!

Meeting Roles

The final step in preparing for your meeting is that of assigning meeting roles to those who will assist you in the meeting. These meeting roles include **Recorder, Facilitator, Participants,** and you as **Leader.** Meet with the Facilitator to discuss his/her role. Meet with the Recorder to let that person know what you expect. Let's consider these meeting roles.

The Leader

1. Start on time to indicate the importance of the meeting and show respect for those who make the effort to be there on time.

2. Create a cordial, yet businesslike atmosphere by clarifying meeting roles and setting up ground rules for the meeting. Ground rules, such as not interrupting other speakers, everyone participates, stick to the agenda, complaints must be accompanied by solutions, no judgments on brainstormed ideas—whatever you think the group needs to do to create an orderly meeting. Create ground rules ahead of time or have participants create them at the beginning of the meeting.

3. Use the agenda throughout the meeting. Start by going over the meeting objective and reviewing the steps of the meeting.

4. Participate as a group member by stating your thoughts during the discussion. Wait to voice yours until after others' statements.

5. Change the format of the meeting if you feel the meeting process is not accomplishing your objective.

6. Summarize key decisions and actions. When Participants arrive at a point or a decision, paraphrase what has transpired.

7. Tell the Recorder what to write on the board or the overhead transparency to record the "group memory."

8. End the meeting on time.

The Facilitator

1. Manage the "people" side of the meeting, so that the Leader can manage the "content" side, by making sure everyone contributes to the discussion, preventing speakers from interrupting others, and protecting people from verbal attacks.
2. Monitor time spent on each agenda item, and keep Leader and Participants within the time frame allotted to that item.
3. Listen for discussion "drift" and get everyone back to the issues at hand. Emphasize the meeting objective, if necessary.
4. Monitor people creating problems and deal with them—tactfully, but directly.
5. Refrain from offering your own opinions. Mediate conflicting opinions.
6. Suggest other approaches when a process isn't working.
7. Take your cues and direction from the Leader.

The Recorder

1. Keep a visual record of the meeting without editing or paraphrasing what people actually say. Don't write until the Leader tells you to!
2. Check regularly with the Leader and Facilitator to ensure accuracy.
3. Try to capture the words expressed, not your interpretation. When in doubt, ask for clarification.
4. Use key words and phrases. Don't try for complete sentences, but do try to capture the complete idea.
5. Keep mental track of what has been said and done, in case the Leader or Facilitator forget or lose track.
6. If note-keeping is stopping the meeting from going forward, ask the Leader to name an assistant. (Large groups may need several of you!)
7. If you use a brown or white board, copy the contents for the Leader or ask another person to copy contents on a sheet of paper.

This role is very important since the results are sometimes the only documentation of what occurred in the meeting. In general, if you are taking minutes which will be copied and sent to participants, include: the date, time, and place of the meeting and those in attendance; agenda items with brief discussions and major contributors; problems discussed and decisions made; action assignments and deadlines. A sample form follows.

Participants

1. Be prepared for the meeting, especially if you have a role to fulfill.
2. Be on time.
3. Participate fully in discussions. Focus on the meeting objective, and help to gain consensus. No social loafing!

4. Listen to others' viewpoints without rushing to judgments based on your biases.

5. Follow the ground rules, and avoid causing meeting distractions.

MEETING MINUTES

Meeting Objective:

Logistics	*Meeting Members*
Date:	1. Leader:
Time:	2. Facilitator:
Location:	3. Recorder:
	4. Attendees:

Agenda Item	Actions	Person Responsible	By When

WHAT DOES A FACILITATOR DO?

Gets everyone to participate
Remains neutral in disagreements
Regulates discussion "traffic"
Focuses group on same issues
Protects people from attack
Monitors time spent on agenda items
Assists Leader in managing the meeting

Leader and Facilitator Actions

Let's differentiate the Facilitator and the Leader roles. First, can one person do both? The answer is yes, but not as well. Results are usually better when the two roles are separated. Meetings are usually shorter and more productive, so that follow-up meetings are fewer. **If you use a Facilitator for several meetings, you will appreciate the difference.** The following suggestions are for Facilitators, but if you don't have one in your meeting, you as Leader should follow these guidelines.

Serve as a discussion traffic director. "Is everyone clear on these directions?" "Trent, hold that thought until we get to that agenda item!" "Have you finished? OK, now it's your turn to talk." "Are we getting anywhere now? Is it time to move on to the next item?" "Hold on; let's talk one at a time. Bill, you first, then Venita, then Patrick."

Command the attention of the group. When a group gets frustrated, walk up close to them to get their attention, then indicate on the overhead or the brown board where the meeting is stalled and suggest a way to move on. If a group is silent, ask whether they're just thinking and need time or whether they need direction. ("Are you asleep or thinking?") Resist being a "ham." You are there to direct the focus of the group, not monopolize the conversation.

Ensure participation. Be positive and encourage people. ("We're doing a good job here; keep going!") Ask quiet people for their input; stop those who dominate groups. ("Thanks, Jill. What do think on this, Jim?")

Restart when things go wrong. If groups get bogged down, take them back to a previous point and encourage them to think in different directions. ("Looks like you're off track and some of you have tuned out. Let's backtrack and redirect the discussion.")

Distinguish between conflict and interpersonal confrontation. People should be listening and reacting to ideas, not focusing on each other's personalities. Even if they seem to be teasing, derisive words linger in the air and in some people's minds. Foul language does, too, so ask people to refrain, even from slang and colloquialisms. ("That's one idea; let's record that. What do other people think?" and "Let's keep the language clean.")

Remember to focus on the meeting. You are in a powerful position when you facilitate. Don't abuse this power. The group came to work, not listen to you, so let the participants do the talking, and don't bask in the limelight. If groups are doing well, step aside and let things happen. You may only have to speak every few minutes, so be brief and concise.

Remain neutral. Even if Participants ask what you think, don't state your views on meeting content. Leaders can state their views; they are dealing with meeting content. Facilitators can't state their views; they're too busy tending the meeting process.

Dealing with Meeting Disruptions

The Facilitator usually has the responsibility of dealing with disruptive or inappropriate behavior, since this is a meeting process issue rather than a meeting content issue. However, if there is no Facilitator, these duties fall to the Leader. In addressing problems during meetings, use a subtle approach initially. People respond to a meaningful glance in their direction or your approaching them to stand directly beside them. If this doesn't work, try some of the vocal interventions listed here.

Latecomers/Early Leavers

Group members may be late sometime. If it's not a usual occurrence, don't disrupt the meeting to review what happened prior to their arrival, unless they are key figures in your meeting. Let the latecomer sit quietly without participating for a while to "catch up" with meeting content. *The Facilitator should supply the latecomer with an agenda, plus any supplies handed out earlier.* If the lateness is chronic, you could try humor by saying, "Sorry, we must have started early." You might also stop the meeting until the latecomer is seated.

Early leavers tend to drain the energy from a meeting. When people leave, others wonder why the meeting continues. When you review the agenda, point out the ending time and ask if anyone has a problem with that. Those with legitimate excuses will usually state them. Courtesy calls for early leavers to speak with you prior to the meeting to apprise you of their need to leave early. You can then work that into your general meeting introduction, so that other participants will be expecting that. If the early leaver will miss an important feature of your meeting which you can't speed up, you should make this clear. They may decide to stay!

Silent/Shy Persons

If silent people are meeting dropouts—reading a newspaper, yawning, rolling their eyes, almost reclining in their chairs—you might consider their purpose in being at the meeting. They may be indifferent to the topic, think the meeting is a waste of time, be bored, or feel that they will have nothing to contribute. One way to get them participating is to stand close to them. Establish eye contact, call them by name and ask them a question. If they don't answer quickly, say, "I'll give you a moment to think" and call on someone else. One thing you should definitely do is ask them to put away their reading material.

On a break, ask them why they are not talking. Just showing them your attention may help them tell you the reason for their behavior, which could be pressing issues at work or preoccupation with other matters. **Other participants will notice how you handle this.**

If silent persons are simply shy, they may look uninvolved, but they are really tracking with you and the meeting content. You can establish eye contact, smile, and ask them an open question—one that needs more than a yes-or-no answer. When they've finished, sincerely thank them to encourage further participation. If you split the class into subgroups, ask silent persons to summarize the discussion. You can also ask a question and have each person in your meeting group respond by sharing their opinions. Interact with them during a break to discover more about their perceptions on the meeting topic; if you can gain their trust, they may contribute more. Silents often process their thoughts deeply, so their responses may not be frequent, but they are nearly always worthwhile.

Whisperers/Side Conversationalists

When you've encouraged people to exchange information and views during a meeting especially by forming subgroups, a few people have trouble "shutting down" once you've called the meeting to order and you want participants to focus their attention in another direction. Whisperers and side conversationalists may not be *consciously* disrupting a meeting; they may just be finishing conversations or adding ideas. Nevertheless, you need a relative amount of silence and cooperation from them. Establishing eye contact sends a subtle message. Standing near them is another step. Stopping the meeting and maintaining silence until they stop talking is a more pointed measure. Asking, "Would you like to share your idea with the whole group?" works as well.

If they persist, they may have a point to make such as an addition to agenda items or a need to voice a perspective not yet aired. You can ask, "Shall we add what you're discussing to the agenda?" Then, *you can make a judgment call* as to whether to give them "air time" then or call another meeting later to address their concerns. If they are simply bored or need to be the center of attention, the steps already mentioned should silence them. The idea is to control these persons so that the meeting progress is not slowed. A number of small conversations going on will disrupt a meeting.

Talk-A-Lots

These people come in several varieties and generally talk too much during your meeting. Their meeting behavior is more inappropriate than disruptive, although one can lead to the other. The important thing to remember in dealing with these types is not to take their behavior personally. They probably behave this way in every meeting they attend, not just yours. Help them become more effective participants with the following strategies.

Loudmouths

Once they have started talking, wait a bit and then ask them, "What's your point?" or, "What's your question?" depending on what you're doing in the meeting. If their responses are vague or unrelated to your meeting topic, you can ask, "How does that relate to our subject?" If they're still talking, say, "Thanks for your comments. Now let's give other people a chance to talk," and call on someone else immediately. If they interrupt, say, "Hold that thought for now, and let Barry finish his statement." If all else fails, look at your watch and call time, either citing the need to move on in the agenda or to hear from the rest of the attendees. If you know in advance of these persons' usual behaviors, you can ask them to take notes during your meeting—for discussion afterwards. They usually don't stick around.

Know-It-Alls

These persons may indeed know a lot about the meeting topic, but they don't contribute in a way that sits well with other participants. They stymie the meeting process and prevent new ideas from being conceived or developed. REMEMBER, IT'S YOUR MEETING, AND YOU ARE LEADING A DELIBERATIVE PROCESS, WHICH MEANS THAT EVERYONE NEEDS TO BE HEARD. When Know-it-alls use their credentials, age, or length of service to disparage an idea, you can say, "We recognize that you've been here a long time, but everyone has a vote on this issue." Another way might be, "We know that you're the expert in this area, but the point of this meeting is to produce new ideas. Do you have any positive ones?" Finally, you can always say, "That's your view; now I'd like to hear from others" and call on someone else. Refuse to speculate with these persons; stick to the facts or experience that you know or call on the expertise of other participants.

If Know-it-alls comment on the meeting process itself by telling you what you should be doing, ask the other participants if they concur. If they say no, then Know-it-alls are at odds with the group, not you. You could also say that there are different ways of approaching problems, there is no one right way, but this is the one that has been selected. If Know-it-alls merely want attention, you will have met that need. If you're aware of these persons' meeting behaviors in advance, you can ask for their support by serving as references during the meeting. If Know-it-alls refuse, at the start of the meeting state their points of view and tell why you disagree, which defuses their arguments. Their biases are showing.

Overall, it's best to get these people on your side or at least going to bat for your team. They may be good resource persons who only want some recognition for their contribution to the company. If, on the other hand, they just **think** they know it all and you know they don't, fail to see their hands when they ask to speak. You could also cite authorities whose credentials supercede those of the Know-it-alls. "I was in a meeting with our president just yesterday, and the message was quite different from your report."

Hostiles/Overly Disagreeables

These persons are unhappy and let the world know that daily or they "show off" by taking issue with everything. Hence they create emotional furor inappropriately in meetings. Some disagreeables get set off by an issue from the meeting itself, which is at least a step in the right direction. You want people to contribute to discussions, but it should be an orderly contribution and others should not be disparaged in the process. Persons arguing on the issues is one thing; persons ridiculing others' physical, mental, or emotional attributes is another.

Infrequently, hostiles do have valid points; they just don't know how to state them constructively. Asking these people to leave your meeting is NOT usually a wise option, so you need to deal with them. If you know about these people in advance of your meeting, you can be prepared for whatever they might say by doing your research and having facts ready to present.

You can also use the defusing technique mentioned earlier, stating at the outset of your meeting that these persons and you disagree. Then you can present your view of the situation, and ask participants to keep an open mind throughout the meeting. This is especially true of topics you know will be controversial. Sometimes the goal of chronically unhappy people is just to get others riled up. They then feel like they've won somehow. Your job is to focus on the issues at hand and not get involved emotionally.

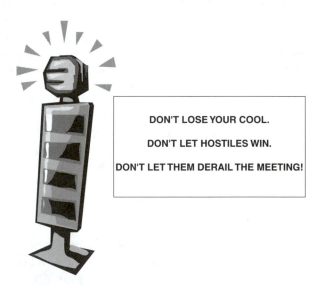

DON'T LOSE YOUR COOL.

DON'T LET HOSTILES WIN.

DON'T LET THEM DERAIL THE MEETING!

When and if hostiles use foul language, disparaging expressions, or negative assessments of situations, don't repeat these terms in your responses. Clean them up or rephrase them to suit your needs. "If you mean welfare mothers, then my response is. . . ." Paraphrase what they say, but delete the expletives and harsh words.

Respond to the content of their statements, rather than the emotional overtones. "Let's make sure we're on the same page. Your major point is that. . . ." You can also agree with something they've said (if you can while maintaining your credibility with the group) and move on to get others' comments. You can also enlist others' support by saying, "That's a unique way of seeing things. Lester, what do you think about that?" When in doubt, boomerang the question or comment to other participants, "Is anyone else interested in talking about this?" If others respond "No," then Hostiles may see that they're outnumbered, and you're off the hook.

You might also say, "You've described a problem for us. What do think is the solution?" This is especially effective if you've written this into your ground rules: don't present a problem unless you also present a solution. Expose the biases of Hostiles and when they pause for breath, ask the group if they want to discuss the Hostile's topic. When they say no, you will be seen as fair and impartial, and the group is pleased to move along in the agenda. After this, you can avoid eye contact and overlook their hands when Hostiles want to be recognized to speak, and the group will support you in this.

If all this fails, see if you can get agreement on a larger issue, especially if the Hostile is differing with smaller details. "We agree then on the big picture, not just the details." You can also just agree to disagree, especially if you've taken time at the beginning to state Hostiles' viewpoints and asked participants to keep an open mind. Of course, you can also check your watch and state that time constraints prevent more discussion, or you can say, *especially* if the group has indicated a lack of interest in Hostiles' topics, that these can be discussed after the meeting. Of course, Hostiles rarely stay after, since their "payoff" is being the center of attention during the meeting.

Finally, you can calmly and directly say, "Mike, your comments are keeping us from accomplishing the purpose of this meeting. I'd appreciate it if you would stop making them." If Hostiles fail to respond to all of these, you have a bigger problem than hostility, and your organization needs to handle that.

In summary, dealing with disruptive and inappropriate behavior in meetings is part and parcel of managing meetings. If you can avoid any of these behaviors by getting to know the people who'll be attending your meeting and understanding their viewpoints and biases, you'll be better prepared to run meetings well.

When and if the behaviors arise, don't be defensive with the disrupters. Arguing with them in heated tones or threatening them places you on their level when you really want to stay above the fray. Also, don't criticize, ridicule, or shame them, especially in front of other participants. If you do, everyone may "shut down" their responses, even though you feel justified. Treat everyone with respect, even Hostiles, even when you're closing off their inappropriate behavior. Honor the person, but not the act.

About Conflict

Many people go to extremes to avoid any sign of disagreement or the appearance of conflict. It is tough for people to learn how to disagree without fighting. In conducting meetings, you hope that conflict will not occur, but if it does, don't be afraid to deal with it. A meeting which airs differences of opinions and exchanges of strongly held beliefs is a good meeting! You got to the heart of matters, and people spoke truthfully. Strong disagreement can generate emotions, but it can also engender deeper thoughts on the issues.

It is important, though, that the opinions and exchanges be controlled, and that's where you come in. Insist that participants stick to the agenda items and the content provided there and prevent personal remarks of any sort. If people bring hidden agendas or unresolved emotional issues to your meeting, contain the contribution of their "baggage" but encourage their thinking and responses to your meeting content.

Be fair;

Be firm;

Bring out the best in people

HANDLING DISRUPTIVE AND INAPPROPRIATE BEHAVIORS HOMEWORK ASSIGNMENT

Directions: Read the assigned material on dealing with disruptive behavior in meetings. Write the requested number of ways to deal with meeting troublemakers on this sheet. Make your suggestions as specific as possible. For example, don't just say "ask a question"; write the question itself. Using your own wording for the ideas helps make this important information your own. Use ideas from your topic.

A. Hostile persons [overly disagreeable] (5 suggestions)

B. Know-It-Alls (3 suggestions)

C. Loudmouths [overly talkative] (5 suggestions)

D. Whisperers [side conversations] (3 suggestions)

E. Silents [quiet, shy] (3 suggestions)

TYPE	SUGGESTED RESPONSE

Example:

Know-It-Alls   *Ask for their support in advance. "I realize you know a lot about this (if they really do). Will you serve as a reference if we need specifics?"*

7

Conducting Problem-Solving Meetings

Introduction

The purpose of a problem-solving meeting is TO FOSTER DISCUSSION of your topic. Most people are not trained for leading participative discussions. Asked to chair a meeting, managers may have no idea how to proceed. Most of the time people fall back on their own experiences, which can be good or bad, but at least it's a guideline, so the thinking goes. This section shows how to lead a discussion so that the meeting objective is achieved, participants have enough "air time" so that they feel their issues have been heard, and managers gather employee input to guide decision making. Meanwhile, remember this!

DO call a meeting when:

- you want information or advice
- you want help solving a problem
- an issue impacts the organization
- problems exist between groups
- you or the groups want to meet.

DON'T call group meetings when:

- you or the bosses have made the decision already
- you can contact the group a more efficient way
- you don't have time to prepare for the meeting
- you don't have enough information to meet
- you need to hire, fire, discuss salary, or evaluate employees!

Most managerial work is conducted through meetings, since meetings function as information-processing systems. People discuss issues and make decisions which, in turn, form organizational policy. Thus, organizations very well may succeed or fail based on the strength of their meetings!

What is a "good" meeting? Issues are discussed, and decisions are made. The decisions are well-considered and require no rework. Plus, those who attend enjoy the process and feel good about their participation, even if their favored view isn't selected as the best choice (Tropman, 1996). *This is the goal of meeting management—having "good" meetings!* Now, if a meeting consists of well-considered decisions in which people participate fully, how do we do the "well-considered" part? Through effective discussions!

Purpose of Problem-Solving Discussion

Discussions vary according to time, circumstance, and people, but universally, they are social activities. Our democratic society favors direct participation due to our national concepts of equality, reasoned thinking, deliberation, and orderly processes. A discussion is *not* a debate, a monologue, or a conversation. It is a cooperative effort in which group members help others study a problem, so there are no winners or losers. It is an interchange with purpose and reason, not a casual conversation. It is systematic in that a steady progression toward a goal takes place. It is creative when people react to opinions and various turns in the discussion. It requires participation through listening and speaking. It calls for leadership so that discussion stays focused, but encourages full expression of viewpoints. Discussion, well-conducted, is a superior way to study a problem.

Discussion calls for reflective thinking—weighing pros and cons, considering alternatives, using logic, considering consequences of possible actions. Groups try to understand the problem and act with a common purpose in solving it. When understanding is the object, participants correct others' thinking or information errors, and all understand that this is for the common good of dealing with the problem (Hyman, 1980).

Problem-solving answers the question "How." In problem-solving discussions, groups seek answers to conflicts or problems facing them. They discuss facts relevant to stated problems and discuss pros and cons of various solutions. Problem-solving discussions truly benefit from many points of view, so fostering a free exchange of ideas is vital. Groups seek ways to correct bad situations, improve current situations, or resolve conflicts between situations or people through discussion. This allows all to hear what others see as workable solutions to problems, PLUS the probable consequences of solutions.

Problem-Solving Meeting Objective

Since the idea here is to get opinions and ideas from others, the meeting objective must reflect this. Meeting objectives start with an infinitive—to do something: to create ways to solve a problem, to gather ideas on an issue, to brainstorm on the impact of decisions already made—a definite "doing" activity. Don't choose wimpy statements, such as "to be aware of" or "to become familiar with"! Be as specific as possible, since the objective tells participants the content and the level of detail to expect in the meeting.

To practice creating problem-solving meeting objectives, go back to the topic selected at the start, look at the three main points covered, and select an idea to use for your problem-solving meeting. Examples follow.

---

1. *Information meeting topic:* To inform about effects of smoking on the job

Key points: 1. Workplace rules concerning smoking
2. Time use/ productivity loss of smokers on breaks
3. Effect on other employees and the organization

Problem-solving meeting objective: To find ways to equalize time use and work produced between smokers and nonsmokers

---

2. *Information meeting topic:* To inform about depression and recovery

Key points: 1. Recognizing depression in yourself and others
2. Treatments for depression (drugs and therapy)
3. Putting your life back together (with help)

Problem-solving meeting objective: To create ways to support depressed people in the workforce

---

3. *Information meeting topic:* To inform about using diet supplements to enhance performance in sports

Key points: 1. Type of supplements available
2. Effect of supplements on sports performance
3. Side effects and long-term use possibilities

Problem-solving meeting objective: To find ways to limit the use of dietary supplements in junior- and senior-high athletes

---

4. *Information meeting topic:* To inform about the depletion of old-growth timber through logging on public lands

Key points: 1. Benefits of old-growth forests
2. Effects of logging on public lands
3. Wood product awareness for consumers

Problem-solving meeting objective: To create ways to provide lumber without using old-growth timber on public lands

---

5. *Information meeting topic:* To inform about consumer credit card debt

Key points: 1. Extent of credit card debt in USA
2. Reasons for mounting debt
3. Effect of debt on the American working class

Problem-solving meeting objective: To create ways to encourage responsible use of credit cards

In thinking about problem-solving meeting objectives, consider what question can be asked that will elicit opinions and ideas from attendees. Don't ask them to repeat back information from the first meeting; ask them an open question—one that requires explanation. If the question has multiple answers that will vary according to the perspective taken, then it's probably a good problem-solving meeting objective.

Leader Role in Problem-Solving Discussion

In general, leaders clarify the meeting objective and decide the structure which follows—ways in which discussion proceeds. However, if groups make suggestions on modifying procedures, leaders can certainly accommodate them. Often groups are content just with being asked. Being consulted by leaders about meeting process increases feelings of commitment to the meeting outcome. Following this, the actual problem-solving discussion takes place. Then, in closing the meeting, leaders ask participants to reach conclusions based on their discussion. Leaders should listen for key ideas and points made during the discussion and RESTATE THESE IN SUMMARY FORM. This calls for skill in leaders, but is quite important in terms of everyone's understanding of group conclusions or recommendations. This is a "big picture" of what transpires in a problem-solving meeting.

The Climate

Discussion leaders are responsible for establishing the correct atmosphere for problem solving. A good climate to establish is one in which respect for persons and opinions is evidenced, and one in which groups cooperate in an open, warm way. Sarcasm, even the kind intended to be humorous, is out of place in this atmosphere, as is anger. *The atmosphere must be positive!* How to ensure this? Establishing ground rules and having a copy posted at each meeting is one part. Introduce people if they don't know one another. Clarify meeting roles. Be positive yourself, rather than complaining about problems. Be prepared for the meeting in terms of supplies and information.

The Agenda

The most important part of presenting meetings is the agenda! At the start of a meeting, review the agenda, making sure the meeting objective is clear and what the expectations are for the meeting. Agendas don't have to be long and formal. Short lists for simple meetings are fine, but if a meeting is fairly complex, the agenda should reflect this. Agendas should be detailed enough that a leader can use them as an outline for conducting the meeting.

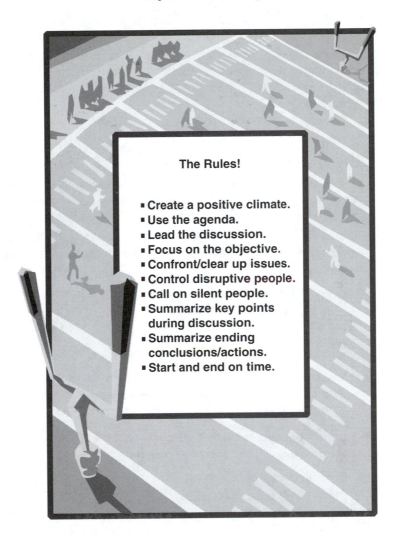

The Rules!

- **Create a positive climate.**
- **Use the agenda.**
- **Lead the discussion.**
- **Focus on the objective.**
- **Confront/clear up issues.**
- **Control disruptive people.**
- **Call on silent people.**
- **Summarize key points during discussion.**
- **Summarize ending conclusions/actions.**
- **Start and end on time.**

The Discussion

The next concern is the downfall of most meetings. With no planning about how a discussion is conducted, most people allow random exchanges of information and commentary, which consume meeting time and result in no accomplishment of purpose. Without clear procedural directions from leaders, attendees may think, "We're going at this all wrong. I want no part of this!" Then they won't accept any decisions made because the procedure seemed flawed, OR they think their input doesn't really matter and stop participating. With either response, meetings and results are not well considered, and meetings-are-a-waste-of-time thoughts begin to work their way into the organizational culture. People who truly are interested in furthering the goals of the organization become frustrated with process and people. It *does* make a difference how groups study problems through discussion! Here are some steps to include.

First establish a basis for the discussion. Have a review of an information meeting, make a prepared statement, give highlights of a written report, ask a resource person to establish facts or reasons, or do some activity that brings a picture to the minds of the attendees. *Clarify the meeting objective!* Examples include, "to solve the problem of . . ." or, "to deliberate the issue of . . ." or, "to consider the pros and cons of. . . ."

Then, use one of the following development ideas:

- If a topic has pros and cons, have two people with known responses speak first; then open the floor to a general discussion.
- Ask someone to make a prepared statement (or make one yourself) and set aside a time *only* for clarification questions. Then follow with a time period for exchanges of agreement or disagreement of participants.
- Ask each participant to make an initial response to the meeting objective, and ask for exchanges from all attendees based on what they've heard.
- If only one differing viewpoint emerges, role play to bring out more.
- Divide the group into subgroups representing differing viewpoints of the problem (customers, employees, management; or teachers, parents, students; or community residents, local administrators, real estate developers). Ask each group to prepare a positional statement and perhaps some questions for others. Then have a general exchange between all people.
- Divide the group into subgroups and ask them to produce an agreed-on number of solutions or recommendations which answer the question posed by the meeting objective. Follow this with a summary of points.

When dividing the whole group into subgroups, provide a list of key questions to answer. Sample questions could ask for:

1. Relevant facts for this stand
2. Key reasons for this stand
3. Probable consequences of the group stand

OR

1. Essential features affecting the view of this group
2. Main causes for the problem from the standpoint of this group
3. Actions which would eliminate the problem
4. Other problems which might occur if particular actions were taken

Depending on your topic, it is possible to inject a bit of humor in subgroups and their vantage points. If the meeting objective is to discuss problems with a cafeteria in an organization, the subgroup representing the chef and the kitchen staff could wear chef's hats or white coats. Food suppliers for the kitchen could wear delivery hats, while supervisors could wear sheriff's posse hats or white ten-gallon hats (to represent the "good guys"). Dressing the part helps establish connection to the role or vantage point being expressed and adds to the *esprit de corps* of the groups. Props can also help make a point: having attendees wear earplugs during a discussion of ways to reduce workplace noise is quite effective.

Discussion Formats

Discussion formats used most often in group meetings are: ordinary group technique, brainstorming, and nominal group technique.

ORDINARY GROUP format is most common. It is an effective way to get a full discussion of the issues, since attendees pay attention to the discussion flow and have easy access to "the floor." Issues get full consideration because of the interactional nature of this meeting process. In ordinary group format, the leader chooses a structure for the meeting and leads the whole group to reach consensus. Without firm leadership, however, things can go wrong: discussion can drag on beyond utility, vocal people can dominate the discussion, members can be swayed by social pressure to agree with the majority opinion rather than sticking up for a minority one. As a result, fewer alternatives may be developed, but in a skillfully led meeting, all sides of the picture are represented, participants feel "heard," and the summary of meeting outcomes truly represents the thoughts and feelings of the group. Success of ordinary group format is highly dependent on the leader's skill and ability to get everyone to participate harmoniously.

BRAINSTORMING is a format which encourages the generation of lots of ideas, some of which may be useful. Rules for this format are:

1. Many ideas should be encouraged.
2. Diverse ideas should be encouraged ("wild, crazy" ideas are OK).
3. "Piggybacking" on each other's ideas should be encouraged.
4. No ideas may be critiqued or criticized.

Participants enjoy brainstorming in small groups (three to five people), but it can also be done in a larger group with a leader (six to ten people). People appreciate being asked for viewpoints and feel a sense of accomplishment in contributing. Brainstorming *sometimes* doesn't produce a large number of ideas in practice, because people self-censor their ideas or fear others will reject them and so don't offer them in the first place. However, this social pressure to conform to majority opinion occurs far less in small groups than in large ones, such as the ones used in ordinary group format. Especially if groups are cohesive, fledgling ideas emerge and are nourished in this format. Groups that work together over time learn the strengths of each member and encourage better idea creation with good nurturing.

It's important here to write down everything anyone says and not comment on the merits of any suggestion. (No killer phrases, like "That's not going to work," or "People will never do that.") It's also important not to think of implementation of ideas, a how-would-our-organization-do-this approach. The sole purpose of brainstorming is to hatch ideas, never mind how popular or doable these may seem initially. Frequently, wild ideas turn out to offer more to the solution than people originally think. Another caveat in brainstorming (and the other formats as well) is not to stop thinking when a good idea emerges. Linear-thinking persons can usually create one or two good ideas, but they have a tendency to think "problem solved!" after this, content with one or two ideas. This is NOT brainstorming in its finest form!

NOMINAL GROUP TECHNIQUE, developed by Andre Delbecq at University of Wisconsin, is a stylized form of brainstorming. Four stages include:

1. Statement of the problem followed by participants individually writing down alternative solutions (semi-adhesive notes are good for this);

2. Participants take turns reporting their ideas while a recorder writes them down or the adhesive notes are grouped according to ideas. This can be done singly or in small groups or in a large group;

3. A brief discussion clears up ambiguities or misunderstandings;

4. Participants are asked to select the best ideas represented. This can be done several ways: participants can be asked to distribute, say, 10 points between their choices, or they could be asked to vote for three choices. If no clear outcome prevails, more discussion is held until consensus emerges.

A variant of this is the *gallery technique*. Individuals' written ideas are copied on a chalkboard or large sheets of paper and participants are given stars or stickers with which to select the best ideas. In essence, they circulate among the ideas rather than the ideas circulating among people (although this happens anyway). Persons selected as discussants in one location could interpret ideas for strolling attendees and perhaps create a summary of thoughts or suggestions as a part of the meeting process. In this version, people enjoy circling the meeting room when several "idea locations" are established, engaging in one-on-one discussions or listening to others weighing pros and cons. Leaders should ensure that the ideas are discussed at some point, either just after they are written individually or after they appear on the large lists, so that all understand each suggestion or idea. Selecting the best ideas for further

ADVANTAGES AND DISADVANTAGES OF DISCUSSION TECHNIQUES

Criteria	Ordinary	Brainstorming	Nominal
Number of ideas	low	moderate	**high**
Quality of ideas	low	moderate	**high**
Social pressure	**high**	low	moderate
Time/money costs	moderate	low	low
Potential for inter-personal conflict	**high**	low	moderate
Feelings of accomplishment	**high**/low	**high**	**high**
Development of "we" feeling	**high**	**high**	moderate

consideration can be done by counting the number of stars or stickers, or having discussants present an overview of comments heard from the strolling participants. In nominal group discussions, people produce a large number of good ideas.

Discussion Focus

Keeping attendees focused on meeting objectives is a major task for leaders. To do this, leaders need practice in contributing to discussions themselves, summarizing the contributions of others, and focusing on meeting outcomes.

Leader contributions can make or break meetings! Leaders must decide beforehand how to contribute to a discussion without dominating it. After all, problem-solving meetings are called to gather group input, not to dispense views held by leaders only. Ask yourself whether you'll be the authoritative resource for the group. Who will track comparisons and explanations? Who will serve as group memory? Who will summarize group thinking on issues? If the answer to these questions is you, then you might well be dominating a meeting, not conducting it. Look at this scenario.

Meeting Objective: To Discuss Implementing the New Call Schedule

Trent, a sales supervisor for a "baby Bell," opened a department meeting for employees making sales calls for the company. For the first five minutes Trent gave performance statistics for the preceding week and asked for questions. No one spoke. Trent then launched the topic of the meeting, which was to examine a new way to schedule sales calls, an idea advanced by a vice president of sales. Trent thought a problem-solving meeting would give employees a chance to troubleshoot potential glitches and to react to the new procedure.

Trent started, "You all received the memo from our vice president about the new calling schedule. This is going to change the way we do business. I have some ideas on how we can work into this new system, but I'd like to get your ideas. Anyone care to contribute?" No one spoke. "OK, here's what I think we should do . . . ," and Trent outlined his plan. No discussion ensued after that, so Trent adjourned the meeting.

When Trent's boss asked how the meeting went, Trent said, "My people never have any ideas at meetings. I give them a chance, but I end up doing most of the talking. They just don't care!"

What is Trent doing wrong? The idea of having this meeting is good, the meeting objective is concisely stated, and attendees had a memo as preparation. *Trent failed to plan and execute a discussion procedure.* One of the discussion development ideas given earlier in this chapter would have worked. For example, Trent could have asked each employee to make an initial response and then ask for exchanges of information and ideas. He could have divided the whole group into subgroups and asked for five or ten suggestions for implementing the new schedule. He could have asked specific questions concerning key implementation problems, causes for these problems, and actions that would eliminate these problems. He could have used any of the three discussion formats: ordinary group, brainstorming, or nominal group. Although Trent's purpose was to conduct a problem-solving meeting, he actually had an information-giving meeting.

Confronting Issues

One way to ensure participation from participants is to assign them roles in the meeting itself. Giving people specific things to do during a discussion maximizes their involvement and improves the quality of the discussion. Having an attendee present a position paper, asking someone to be the first speaker after your introduction, asking someone to serve as resource person, assigning the responsibility for summarizing periodically and/or recapitulating discussion results at the end, asking others to keep track of time spent, to record meeting transactions, and to greet/seat people as they arrive are all ways to improve discussion structure.

The Meeting Roles chapter delineated four activity roles: Leader, Facilitator, Recorder, and Participant. In leading problem-solving meetings, use at least a Facilitator and Recorder.

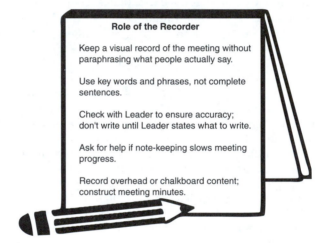

Role of the Recorder

Keep a visual record of the meeting without paraphrasing what people actually say.

Use key words and phrases, not complete sentences.

Check with Leader to ensure accuracy; don't write until Leader states what to write.

Ask for help if note-keeping slows meeting progress.

Record overhead or chalkboard content; construct meeting minutes.

A Facilitator's sole purpose is to ensure a smoothly run meeting. Facilitators can do the "heavy lifting" during a meeting. Leaders can ask them to do whatever needs doing, but their customary roles are detailed in the first graphic on page 69. Good Facilitators are observant, noticing the silents or shys in groups and asking for their opinions or participation. Facilitators should have the moxie to tell authority figures if they are breaking ground rules and when they have a turn in speaking. Among peer groups, Facilitators will call for quiet in a meeting, block dominators from affecting group members, gain cooperation from reluctant participants, and shut down silly behavior. In problem-solving meetings, Facilitators will listen in on group discussions to make sure they are on track with the meeting objective. They can also carry a portable microphone to speakers in the meeting. They can conduct some steps in the meeting if the Leader asks. For example, they can coordinate participation in the gallery technique by keeping people moving, ensuring that all suggestions are included, and asking people to speak up if their voices are too soft for all to hear. Facilitators may be asked their opinions, but since they are supposed to be unbiased, good ones will decline answering.

A caveat here is a caution against acting like a militant constituent when facilitating meetings. None of the foregoing activities needs to be done in an unpleasant or unnecessarily abrupt manner. Smile and use a pleasant voice. Be firm, fair, and consistent in dealing with people.

Role of the Facilitator

1. Manages the meeting *process* so that Leader is free to manage meeting *content;*
2. Listens for discussion "drift"; refocuses on meeting purpose;
3. Deals with disruptive and inappropriate behavior;
4. Mediates conflicting opinions; does NOT voice own opinions;
5. Suggests other approaches when one isn't working;
6. Monitors time spent on agenda items;
7. Takes directions from Leader.

Now, what does a Leader actually do when it comes to contributing to discussions, summarizing the contributions of others, and focusing on meeting outcomes? First, please know that a Leader can't just sit back and let whatever happens happen. The Leader is conducting an ensemble of participants by interacting and being attentive and prepared to participate.

When meeting attendees ask for information or an opinion, Leaders should contribute. The art comes in not contributing too much or too often. The center of attention should be the participants themselves and the intellectual task which lies before them.

Leaders can lend their expertise by

♦ providing needed information, if an essential point is being left out;

♦ correcting critical errors that others don't correct;

♦ responding to requests;

♦ offering a new way to view a problem under discussion.

Especially when confronting and clearing up issues, Leaders should offer mini-summaries of the discussion from time to time (or designate someone to do this). After several people have spoken about a problem segment, condense what has been said or indicated by body language or tone of voice. Reflect the emotions described *and* the content. This has the effect of crystallizing the thought processes, sometimes giving participants common terminology which they can use to further the discussion. To do this:

- clarify points made by people;
- reflect the impact of their remarks;
- offer alternative meanings for speakers' comments.

In doing this, try to find merit in others' ideas, make sure you understand others' main points, and check your understanding by stating their views back to them without implying criticism. Don't interject your own ideas until you have fully understood what others have said.

In summarizing the contributions of others, Leaders must be good listeners and be skilled in helping people express themselves. One way to do both is to ask questions. Here are some questioning techniques:

- Testing the water to discover the group's feelings:
  "What would your reaction be if we went to this new system?"
- Getting participation from the group:
  "We've heard from Kent and Kristen. What do the rest of you think?"
- Getting specific facts:
  "What were our final sales figures last month? Does anyone have this?"
- Getting the reluctant attendee to talk:
  "John, you've been here for ten years. What do you think of these ideas?"
- Clarifying/elaborating on someone's point:
  "Can you give more information on that issue?" or, "Are you saying. . . ."

Focusing meeting outcomes is another task of Leaders in confronting and clearing up issues. Sometimes discussion drifts so gradually, it's hard to recognize. However, a Leader must not only recognize it, but put it back on its intended course or direct it on another path that seems desirable. The Facilitator can assist in detecting meeting drift also. Both must keep in mind the meeting objective and the point of the discussion.

Leaders can connect previous statements or summaries with current ones to direct the meeting toward a specific focus. It's important that Leaders give reasons for refocusing on the original objective or emphasizing a different part of the meeting purpose. This makes logical sense to participants and keeps everyone posted on current deliberations. If a group is "spinning its wheels," repeating the same ideas without advancing the discussion, Leaders can make a negative statement or exclude something that is not adding to the discussion. "We won't consider that aspect of the problem now, but we do have time to talk more about. . . ." In this way, Leaders make spur-of-the-moment decisions based on an overall plan for the meeting and the needs of the attendees.

Encourage lots of ideas and consider differences of opinion as creative opportunities. When you disagree or have another opinion, state it, but once you've made your point, don't harp on it. Don't get vested in your own position, but don't support ideas you can't live with, either. Above all, don't get overly emotional; maintain a sense of calm and reason, even when exchanges become heated.

In guiding meeting focus, Leaders should:

- keep the discussion going in planned directions, *always trying to make progress in discussion,* rather than rehashing issues
- set limits on what can be discussed
- connect the needs of participants to the overall discussion plan

Questions to ask in focusing /refocusing are:

- "We've heard all the cons of the new system. What are some pros?"
- "Let's stop discussing this one aspect and consider instead how this new system will affect quality."
- "What would happen if. . . . ?"
- "We've discussed this issue pretty thoroughly. Are you ready to move on to issues we haven't talked about yet?"

- Provide needed information; correct errors
- Offer new ways to view problems
- Offer mini-summaries from time to time
- Clarify points and reflect the impact of remarks
- Restate views of others to check understanding
- Find merit in others' ideas
- Ask questions to help others express thoughts
- Focus on meeting objective/point of discussion
- Exclude ideas that do not add to discussion
- Make progress in discussions
- State your viewpoints and listen to others'
- Remain calm and reasonable in exchanges
- Summarize group conclusions; seek agreement
- Determine further actions/implementation

Ground Rules

The next items in THE RULES have been discussed in previous chapters. The negative behaviors that disrupt meetings are familiar and must be dealt with when they occur in meetings. Some of these behaviors are:

- attacking people and their ideas
- competing for group attention with boasting

- dominating "air time"
- horsing around or clowning
- making irrelevant comments
- speaking sarcastically
- going off on tangents
- withdrawing by acting indifferent

Some of these behaviors can be checked by establishing and enforcing ground rules. Ground rules establish ahead of time what is expected of attendees. If people tend to talk among themselves a lot at meetings, make a ground rule about speaking only when called on by the Leader. If people tend to go on and on and on once they start speaking, limit each speaker to one minute at a time and have the Facilitator keep track of time and silence speakers once the time limit is met. Some people tell "war stories" or recite "pity party" tales ("bitch" sessions) when they meet, so make a ground rule that no problems are brought up for discussion without presenting solutions. Eliminate personal agenda discussions; these occur when a person or persons have a singular viewpoint and keep expressing it over and over in different ways. Once they've been heard, keeping refocusing on the meeting objective itself and stop calling on these people unless they offer new insights. Also, rule out "they" statements in attributing blame. Finally, insist on no killer phrases, belittling remarks, and abrupt subject shifts. Control your meeting through ground rules. A sample follows.

1.   Arrive and start on time.

2.   Be there and be prepared to meet.

3.   Be responsible for following these ground rules.

4.   Stick to the agenda.

5.   Listen to all people respectfully and respond thoughtfully.

6.   No interruptions, side conversations, killer phrases, etc.

7.   No social loafing or silent attendees.

8.   Use appropriate humor selectively.

9.   Work for consensus in making major decisions.

10. Accept responsibility for meeting roles and duties.

Summarizing the Discussion

Finally, THE RULES call for ending the meeting appropriately. If you have achieved the goals of the meeting or if people run out of energy or interest or if you run out of time, close the meeting. It's better, however, to have your Facilitator track time well enough that you have sufficient time to close the meeting in an unhurried fashion.

Leave time in the agenda for the end phase. A discussion without an appropriate end leaves participants with uncertainty about what they accomplished, plus a feeling of dissatisfaction. Also called *closure*, ending a meeting or closing discussion calls for a recapitulation of the key points of the discussion. The Recorder can do this, provided the Leader has asked periodically for recording of mini-summaries. Leaders can also ask participants to draw conclusions, and the Leader can summarize as well.

In summarizing, define areas of agreement and disagreement between people or groups and synthesize the major ideas advanced into five alternatives you can take into your next meeting, decision-making.

Synthesizing means looking at everyone's suggestions and deciding which ones represent the major ideas of the participants. If there is a minority opinion, decide how this can be expressed. If there is general disagreement about ideas advanced, consider how to phrase the major outcomes so that the diverging ideas or opinions are clearly included. This is especially important when differing viewpoints from the factions involved in the problem have been considered. For example, customers, employees, and management may have very different ideas about solving a problem common to all. The summary demands that Leaders think on their feet!

In closing a discussion, Leaders should convey a sense of firmness so that attendees know this is the final overview, not a bid to open up more discussion. If interaction occurs at this stage, people lose their focus because they are hearing that the meeting is over. They've closed their mental notebooks and are thinking of their jobs, or what they're having for dinner, or where the nearest bathroom is; they don't want to reopen the discussion.

Another tip is to make the closing quick. Don't take this time to fill the group in on personal perspectives, and so on. Be brief in opening AND closing. A final act can be to ask the participants where they want to go from here—suggested activities for the future, or a to-do statement. Complimenting the group for providing excellent points for discussion is in order. Then, true to your word, close the meeting.

Problem-Solving Meeting Example: Neighborhood Park at Risk

Background

It's springtime, and a neighborhood park in a Midwestern city of 50,000 is having problems. The Parks Superintendent, Al Smith, has informed Park Board members about acts of vandalism: posts and railings are being ripped from bridges, graffiti is being painted on benches, and off-road bikes are ridden over grassy banks, making trails and causing erosion. Local police caught four juveniles shooting pellet guns at hikers at the park and discovered three other youths rappelling from the Hundred Foot Bridge over Crow Creek. (Rappelling had been heavily discouraged after a youngster fell, injuring himself seriously two years ago.) Finally, residents of a nearby subdivision are depositing tree limbs and grass clippings near the park entrance, and realtors are using the entrance way to post "FOR SALE" signs.

Al Smith also pointed out a project offer made by a Boy Scout earning his Eagle Scout badge. Andrew Pike asked the Board if he could landscape a parking lot and entryway to a new trail in the park and presented a plan for flowers, plants, and trees.

A problem-solving session is called for! First, consider what the meeting objective should be. Is it to deal with each individual problem or would an overall approach work better? Think about these things: what is the problem, who is responsible for dealing with the problem, what is causing the problem, what actions would eliminate the problem, and what other problems may occur if particular actions are taken. A good meeting objective might read: *to create a list of solutions for our neighborhood park problems.* Then create an agenda for this problem-solving meeting.

The minutes for the meeting reflected the action discussed. The issue discussion yielded the result that the problem was caused by young people in the park, especially at night, a lack of supervisory "presence," and flagging community support for the park. The Town Board accepted responsibility for pursuing solutions. The brainstorming produced these:

Rappelling from bridge
- make it unlawful
- fence entire park
- use security cameras
- bridge attendant
- build climbing wall

Destroying bridge railings/posts
- reinforce posts/railings
- install steel or concrete p/r
- put electric charge on rail
- better lighting
- volunteer patrols

Pellet-gunning hikers
- community service for guilty
- forbid hiking on trails
- patrol hiking areas
- warning signs for hikers
- arm hikers (in some way)

Biking on hills/causing erosion
- designate bike paths/trails
- barriers on eroded areas
- loose gravel on eroded areas
- plant flowers & trees in area
- sprinkler system

MEETING AGENDA

Meeting Objective: To create a list of solutions for our neighborhood park problems

---

Logistics

		Group Members:	
Date:	*May 10*	*1. Leader:*	*Al Smith*
Time:	*7:00 PM*	*2. Facilitator:*	*Messina Alvarez*
Location:	*Town Hall*	*3. Recorder:*	*Frank Corvin*
		4. Attendees:	*Town Board members*
Meeting called by:	*Al Smith*	*Phone:*	*765.000.000*

Agenda Item	Process	Time	Person Responsible

1. Opening
    Meeting roles
    Process overview
	Lecture	2 min.	Al Smith (AS)
			
			Messina Alvarez

2. Overview of problems
    Shooting hikers with
      pellet guns
    Rappelling on bridge
    Destroying bridge
      rails & posts
    Bikes making trails
    Graffiti on benches
    Yard waste at entrance
    Real estate ad signs
	Blackboard	1 min.	AS & Frank Corvin

3. Discussion of issues
    Problem causes?
    Whose responsibility?
	Ordinary group	5 min.	AS, MA, FC &
			    Town Board

4. Listing solutions	Ordinary group brainstorming	10 min.	(Same)
5. Selecting best solutions (at least five)	Ordinary group	5 min.	(Same)
6. Discussion of impact	Ordinary group	3 min.	(Same)
7. Summary of meeting actions	Interactive lecture	1 min.	AS
8. Setting decision-making meeting date & closing	Interaction	1 min.	AS & Board

Graffiti on benches
  remove benches
  build "graffiti wall"
  night patrols
  local artists paint benches
  adopt-a-bench program

Real estate signs
  tell realtors no signs
  put up NO SOLICITING signs
  time limits for advertising
  realtors sponsor park signs: no biking, etc.
  realtors sponsor vests for volunteers

Dumping yard wastes
  increased lighting at entrance
  guard dogs
  surveillance cameras
  recycling/compost area
  yard waste pickup at homes

After the brainstorming portion of the meeting, Frank Corvin noted that some solutions were positive and some were negative. He suggested that unrealistic solutions, such as putting an electric charge on bridge rails be eliminated and that solutions which were positive and involved community effort to accomplish be used in the final list of solutions. The final list:

1. A call for public participation
     Adopt-a-spot program for bridge, trails, and benches
     Form a citizens' watch program with volunteers from all age groups
2. Facilities improvement
     Increase lighting in park
     Designate bike trails and construct barriers for bikes on eroded areas
     Sponsor bench-painting contest with local artists or school children
     Establish a park curfew/closing time; police patrol at night
3. Community services cooperation
     Police patrol outside park perimeter for pellet-gun shooters
     Community service for juvenile offenders—park maintenance
     Realtors sponsor vests to identify volunteers on duty
     Enact ordinance to make bridge rappelling illegal
     Encourage service organizations (Lions, Kiwanas, church groups) to
       sponsor more youth activities in the community
     Yard waste pick up in subdivision

During the discussion of impact of these solutions, the participants voiced their satisfaction with a positive approach to problems. Since budget concerns were an issue, the Board felt effective, but not costly solutions could be found. They discussed encouraging more Boy Scout projects, similar to Andrew Pike's. They realized that involving the community would require their coordinating efforts and more meetings at Town Hall, but they felt they could do that. Finally, they agreed to get information on implementation and meet again to decide which ideas to implement first.

Problem-Solving Meeting Practice: Saving Adolescents

Bad grades, defiant attitudes, odd clothes, withdrawal from school activities, little communication with parents—typical teen behavior or warning signs? After a nine-year study, The Carnegie Council on Adolescent Development reported that the nation is neglecting young adolescents to the extent that half of our 19 million+ population may not be able to lead productive lives!

The report, *Great Transitions* (1995), focused on 10- to 14-year-olds which a 27-member panel of scientists, scholars, and others described as being most in need of guidance and support at a time when parents and society find dealing with them perplexing. Children entering adolescence try to become more independent through new behavior and activities just when parental involvement in school and their influence in young lives decrease. Three-fourths of parents surveyed stated high and medium involvement with their nine-year-olds, while more than half make this claim with 14-year-olds.

Recommendations of the report? Parents need to maintain their involvement with young teens with the help of their employers in creating time to do this. Youth groups need to reach out to adolescents. Schools could better meet the developing needs of this age group, and health professionals should be better attuned in order to treat them. Finally, the media needs to tone down violence, sex, and drug use by emphasizing the downside of these, rather than glamourizing them.

Add to this a contribution from Joseph Califano, Director of the National Center on Addiction and Substance Abuse, that details which teens are more or less likely to use drugs.

Teens least likely to use drugs

- They eat dinner with the family at least six days a week.

- They are concerned about doing well in school.

- They regularly attend worship services with their parents.

- They feel that drug use is morally wrong.

- They attend schools where there is little or no access to drugs.

- They have friends who do not drink, smoke, nor use drugs.

Teens more likely to use drugs

Their families rarely eat dinner together.

They aren't given a specific curfew.

They don't attend worship services with their families.

Their parents smoked marijuana and their teens know it.

Their parents assume their kids will experiment with drugs.

Their parents blame society, the media, and teens' friends for teens' use, not themselves.

Your assignment: Create a meeting agenda, complete with objective, for a problem-solving discussion of these issues. Choose a discussion format, and plan a meeting which should produce a consensus of five specific suggestions for your community. Practice conducting this meeting with a group of friends or persons interested in this topic.

AGENDA FOR PROBLEM-SOLVING MEETING

Meeting Objective:

Logistics	*Meeting Members*
Date:	1. Leader:
Time:	2. Attendees:
Location:	Meeting called by:
	Phone:

Agenda Item	Process	Time	Who's Responsible

Outline for Problem-Solving Meeting

Opening Figure out an interesting opening, just as you did earlier. Then reintroduce yourself; remind participants of your topic and why they should be interested in it (What's in it for them?). (30 sec.)

Background State your objective and outline previous meetings. (1 min.)

Topic Statement State your problem-solving meeting objective. Then describe the problem thoroughly, giving attendees sufficient information that they can produce viable ideas. (1–2 min.)

Preview Reveal your plan for conducting the discussion (what format, group designation, time limits for discussion) and what all should do when they finish. (1–2 min.)

Body Signal small groups to start OR start discussion yourself if you are using the ordinary group technique. If small-group discussion techniques are used, allow time for groups to report the results of their discussions. Visit each group to check progress and understanding and ask for questions.

When allotted time is up, call groups to order and ask them to report/record their suggestions so that total group can hear/see. If using ordinary group technique, ask whole group to come up with suggestions. (Time dependent on topics.)

Connectives Keep discussion moving, and continually relate what is said back to the problem. **Don't let the discussion drag.**

Conclusion Synthesize areas of consensus or disagreement. As participants talk, try to understand what they are suggesting and TELL YOUR RECORDER WHAT TO WRITE. Compose five alternatives for use in the decision-making meeting (with the help of attendees). Repeat the selections and ask for agreement. Adjourn meeting.

AGENDA FOR PROBLEM-SOLVING MEETING

Meeting Objective:

Logistics	*Meeting Members*
Date:	1. Leader:
Time:	2. Attendees:
Location:	Meeting called by:
	Phone:

Agenda Item	Process	Time	Who's Responsible

PROBLEM-SOLVING MEETING CRITIQUE

LEADER: **OBSERVER:**   **PTS. POSSIBLE: 45**

PREPARATION:

Professional appearance   (3) _____

Detailed agenda   (3) _____

PRESENTATION:

OPENING:	Attention-getting opener	(1) _____
	Reintroduce self & topic	(1) _____
BACKGROUND:	Previous talk (3 main points)	(1) _____
TOPIC STATEMENT:	Fully describe problem/importance	(5) _____
PREVIEW:	Tell how discussion will be conducted (time limits? groups? overall plan?)	(3) _____
BODY:	Conduct discussion	
	Encourage participation from all	(1) _____
	Keep discussion moving	(1) _____
	Summarize viewpoints periodically	(3) _____
	Elicit opinions/alternatives from all	(2) _____
	Synthesize consensus or disagreement	(3) _____
CONCLUSION:	Ask group for five major alternatives	(3) _____
	Memorable close to meeting	(2) _____

PERFORMANCE:

	Enthusiasm/vitality/creativity	(4) _____
	Use of visual aids	(2) _____
	Use of Recorder	(1) _____
	Use of Facilitator	(3) _____
	Time management (15–20 minutes)	(3) _____

TOTAL POINTS EARNED

Comments:

OBSERVATION SHEET
for Problem-Solving Meeting

PRESENTER: OBSERVER:

5—Excellent   4—Good   3—Average   2—Needs work   1—Poor

PERSONAL PREPARATION

	5	4	3	2	1
1. Appropriate business attire	5	4	3	2	1
2. Voice quality/tone	5	4	3	2	1
3. Voice audibility	5	4	3	2	1
4. Confident posture/behavior	5	4	3	2	1

PRESENTATION PREPARATION

	5	4	3	2	1
5. Good organization	5	4	3	2	1
6. Meaningful topic/key point development	5	4	3	2	1
7. Attention-getting opening/closing	5	4	3	2	1
8. Easy-to-follow delivery	5	4	3	2	1
9. Rehearsed performance	5	4	3	2	1

PROJECTION

	5	4	3	2	1
10. Vocal effectiveness (intonation, fillers, pauses)	5	4	3	2	1
11. Audience interaction/eye contact	5	4	3	2	1
12. Energy/enthusiasm portrayed	5	4	3	2	1

STRONG POINTS: WORK ON:

PROBLEM-SOLVING MEETING SELF-CRITIQUE/
SINGLE CONFERENCE REPORT

Name:

General Topic:

Problem for group discussion:

Watch your video of the meeting; type your responses on a separate sheet. Discuss these questions; don't just answer yes or no.

1. After watching your video, comment on the visual impression you give and the nonverbal image you project. (plus and minus)

2. How clear are you in introducing yourself, reminding people of your previous talk, and establishing the problem imbedded in your topic? What could you have done better?

3. How did your discussion go? After your instruction, were the participants clear on what they were to do?

4. Did you keep the discussion moving and relevant to the problem? Did you relate participants' comments back to the problem?

5. How well did you define and synthesize areas of consensus and/or disagreement?

6. What do you want to work on next time?

Conducting Decision-Making Meetings

Introduction

Most people are not trained for group participation and decision making, yet day after day we sit in meetings to air a few sides of complex issues and then vote on implementation—and may the most vocal contingent win! Many automatically consider group decisions as poor ones, or at least worse than decisions made by individuals. When decisions are processed without being well considered, the results *are* likely to be poor. Wait a minute! Wasn't the last chapter about issues being well considered? Yes, discussion starts with problem solving—and continues in decision making. This section shows some specifics of decision making and polishes the discussion skills developed thus far by emphasizing questioning techniques and developing criteria for making good decisions.

Advantages of Group Decision Making

Johnson and Johnson in *Joining Together: Group Theory and Group Skills* define effective group decisions as having these characteristics:

1. the resources of group members are fully realized;
2. time is well used;
3. the decision is correct or of high quality;
4. the decision is implemented fully by all the required group members;
5. the problem-solving ability of the group is enhanced, or at least not lessened (1997, p. 228).

These authors cite studies that illustrate the power of group decision making. The first advantage is that of "process gain," in which interacting with others causes most people to think new thoughts that they wouldn't have had by considering the issue individually (p. 232). The second advantage is that thinking errors or blind spots can be more easily recognized and addressed by groups. A third advantage is that groups have more accurate recall of events or factual information than individuals. A fourth advantage is that groups encourage achievement by members helping one another and giving encouragement. Humans just try harder when others give social support and cooperation! Competitiveness, fear of punishment, and embarrassment are lessened by group membership. Called "social facilitation," this process strengthens group decision making.

A fifth advantage is that involving others in decision making increases commitment in implementing the decisions that are made. Through discussion, people learn new information which may cause them to modify their opinions. They also hear persuasive arguments that may cause them to reconsider the issues. Especially if brainstorming has occurred, unique ideas may be brought to light. Additionally, people discern in discussion thoughts and impressions that are common to all in the group, so that underlying issues and ideas become apparent. Plus, in discussion, people's training and experiences add to the resources available to the group.

So what's not to like about group decision making! *Well conducted*, group discussions and subsequent decisions can change attitudes and behavior in people. Process determines outcome. Being able to conduct decision-making meetings is a powerful tool in meeting management!

Leader Role in Decision-Making Discussion

Remember why leaders call meetings? Primarily, they want information or advice or help solving a problem. In other words, input is needed from workers. If it is being done right, members will efficiently use their resources (work information, experience, special skills or knowledge) to arrive at high quality decisions that will be implemented fully. This is a tall order!

How does leader behavior figure in this scheme? Leaders can succeed or fail based on their meeting behavior! An authoritative person who admonishes or lectures a group and then asks for a decision can expect little effort in implementation. Add a little arrogance or insensitivity to the mix and leaders stir up resentment, as well. Guess what happens to implementation efforts! A participative leader who listens and encourages a group to arrive at its own conclusions can expect implementation of decisions without much further ado. Meeting leaders need to decide which results are desired.

Is an authoritative position always wrong? No! When decisions don't require committed action from group members, or when coordination of members' activities is simple and easy, or when decisions have to be made quickly, an authoritative role is appropriate. So don't think that the ONLY way to make decisions is to arrive at consensus! In the situations just mentioned, leaders go and do. However, if quick implementation and good morale are integral to a decision, leaders should use participative styles.

Kurt Lewin (1951) did classic experiments during World War II to discover how to change people's attitudes and behaviors. Good cuts of meat were in short supply, so shoppers were encouraged to buy kidneys and sweetbreads. Those who promised aloud to buy the less desirable cuts carried through their verbal commitment at far greater rates than those who promised privately. Another study asked college students to set goals for their reading and exam scores. Half verbalized their commitment; half did not. At mid-semester, the publicly committed students averaged 86-percent improvement compared to 14-percent improvement of others. Spoken commitment helps to change behavior and attitudes. Further, when consensus is felt in groups, social support for changing is enhanced. This is why group decision making is important to organizations and to leaders.

Gaining Consensus

How do meeting leaders get others to commit verbally to new behaviors? Through consensus! It's defined as *group solidarity in sentiment and belief*. In practice, distinguishing between consensus and majority rule is sometimes difficult. Majority vote is probably the most common group decision-making procedure used today. Most people consider it democratic since it resembles our election system—51 percent of the vote wins. The problem is that the other 49 percent may feel a sense of loss and feel compromised. Arguments may occur just for the sake of argument, rather than having a basis in reasoning, and knowing they are in the minority causes some people to withhold their resources from groups. They may be in a position to sabotage implementation as well.

Achieving consensus takes longer, but it is more effective if everyone's contributions are needed for implementation. Even *a degree* of consensus can be superior to majority vote. In consensus, it is important that everyone in the group feels he or she had a fair chance at influencing the final outcome. This means that sufficient time was allowed for all to state their views, all felt understood, opposite views were heard, and ultimately all will support whatever decision is made. When differences arise, groups will ask for more information, clarify issues, and try for a better outcome.

Group leaders should encourage airing opposing viewpoints and the reasoning and information behind these viewpoints. They must encourage all members to participate, discourage "giving in" to opposing viewpoints just to avoid conflict, and express acceptance of differing viewpoints, especially minority views. The challenge is to get the group to come up with a decision which all can support. Create a sense of gain, not loss! People will feel senses of unity and personal ownership in the decisions made.

GAINING CONSENSUS
(getting all to feel they had a fair chance to influence the outcome)

- Allow time for all to state their views.
- Ensure understanding of all views.
- Encourage opposing viewpoints.
- Clarify reasoning and information for viewpoints.
- When differences occur, clarify issues and gather information; try for a better consensus statement.
- Discourage "giving in" just to avoid conflict.
- Arrive at a decision all can support.
- Create a sense of gain, not loss!

Clearly, leader behavior and meeting conduct are important to people in organizations as they carry out decisions that are made. How to ensure that everyone feels heard and viewpoints are stated and clarified? Ask questions!

Asking Questions

An important skill for meeting leaders is that of questioning in order to draw out ideas and information and to involve participants in a meeting. Leaders must *probe* to get at ideas, *support* participants when they make contributions, and *listen* attentively as people talk.

PROBING involves asking speakers:

- to clarify ideas or to state examples of what seems vague;
- to explain how the speaker arrived at the position taken;
- to supply causes or purposes for specific suggestions;
- to supply possible consequences of suggested actions;
- to suggest ways to implement proposed solutions.

The most common probe is "Why." Avoid using this on personal matters, of course, since the answer might be embarrassing. Try not to threaten anyone when asking them to supply more information. Just ask for clarification—"Do you mean . . . ?" and then, "What would be the consequences of that?" Asking how a suggestion relates to other issues under consideration is another useful probe. Also asking respondents to make generalizations from their statements helps others to understand their positions better.

Leaders asking questions cause meeting attendees to respond. Don't ask so many questions, however, that the meeting resembles an interrogation. Plan your questions in advance and keep them at a minimum, since the hope is that attendees themselves will ask some questions. If leaders question too much, people are talking to them, not one another, which is the idea of a discussion. People need to talk to each other to agree or disagree with a point, to add information to a statement made, or to raise a question themselves.

Questions are important in getting attention, maintaining interest, and receiving feedback. When leaders ask questions, they can determine the comprehension, understanding, and agreement of participants. Don't ask questions when you already know the answers. Ask the attendees questions that call on their experiences or their opinions. Make your first ones easy to answer, just to get the information-sharing ball rolling!

Goal	Questions to Ask
To get information	Begin with "what, where, when, why, who, how, and how much."
To broaden discussion	How would you do that? How would that help the problem? What things should we think about?
To verify information	Where did you hear that? Have you tried this?
To test assumptions	What would happen if we tried this? If we do it differently, will it work?
To voice your opinion	Would this idea work? Would you be willing to try this?
To reach agreement	Which of these plans do you like? Which idea can we all support? Do we all agree this is what we want?

(Lippincott, 1994, p. 129)

SUPPORTING is a nonverbal as well as verbal skill. When leaders encourage participation from shy or silent persons, praise people for words or actions, or relieve tension with humor, they are supporting participants. Making eye contact, smiling at people, and focusing discussion on someone's response to a question tell attendees that they are doing fine and their contributions are appreciated. Another way to support groups as they participate in meetings is through listening.

WRONG WAYS TO LISTEN

- **Agreeing**
  Nodding your head or saying "Uh huh" after every statement made.
- **Rehearsing**
  Thinking about what you want to say while others are speaking.
- **Daydreaming**
  Letting your mind wander while others talk.
- **Switching**
  Changing the subject back to your own focus when a speaker finishes.
- **Arguing**
  Focusing on something to ridicule or to judge.
- **Personalizing**
  Relating everything the person says to your own life or focusing on a "hidden" message, rather than what the person is saying.

Good listening means that leaders should be able to repeat back everything others have said, plus understanding their feelings about the subject. Check with others by saying, "What I heard you say was. . . . Is that right?" If a lot of emotion came out with the words, reflect the emotion: "You really sound frustrated!" These steps make people feel heard, along with the open-forum effect of speaking candidly within a group. When others are speaking, don't play with a pen or fidget and try not to interrupt them, even though you may sense what they are about to say. Being attentive tells folks that what they're saying is important—it's worth listening to.

"I try to listen. . . . Yeah, I think I do that!"

Kristen, in Accounting, says, "Time is money," and does ledgers while people are in her office because it saves time. "They must have time to burn!" A junior accountant scheduled a meeting to discuss standard costs that he thought could be reduced. Kristen had a better idea, so she jumped right in and set everyone in the meeting straight. Expecting thanks for helping with a new idea, Kristen was surprised when her boss said, "Kristen, sometimes people feel you don't listen to them." "I think I listen," Kristen mused, wondering how to get better at this.

Listening is active, not passive! Face speakers and make eye contact, bending or leaning toward them slightly. Take notes or have a Recorder take notes as you dictate, and wait three to five seconds after people finish before speaking, which assures them that no one is waiting anxiously to talk. Follow the content being discussed, smile when something is humorous, nod in agreement from time to time. Listen noncritically; hear speakers out and check for understanding before discussing their messages. "I'd really like to hear more about the plant meeting. Do you have a few more minutes?" "I hadn't thought of doing it that way. Guess we should check with your area first. Any other ideas we should know about?"

Clarify what people say to be sure exactly what speakers mean. Ask questions or rephrase an unclear statement and ask if the restatement is correct. "In other words, people are quitting because of this problem?" "Normal turnaround has been 48 hours; you're saying it now takes longer?" While listening, begin putting what's said into your own words, so that the *meaning* of it is clear. Then give speakers a chance to correct misunderstandings. "I guess I missed your point. You don't dislike the new policy, but you do think implementation time and cost will be excessive. Is that closer to your meaning?"

Questioning Techniques

In groups of 30 or fewer people, these are techniques for questioning:

- Name response—make eye contact, call the person by name, and ask a question;
- Delayed name response—ask a question of the whole group, then call on a person by name;
- Boomerang—someone in the group asks a question and you redirect it to the whole meeting group or a specific person;
- Back-at-you—rephrase a question asked and direct it back to the person who asked.

Try to use names, rather than "Hey, you!" in essence. Use name tents or a seating chart, something to personalize your meeting.

In larger groups, more than 30, encourage short answers and hint at an answer to get people involved:

- Fill-in-the-blanks—Ask a question of the entire group, such as "What is the customer service goal for our company?" or, "What is our mission in business?" You can also ask for a show of hands on an issue.

- Multiple choice—Ask a question and supply two or three alternatives for the participants, such as, "How many acres of land in the public domain exist in America? 10,000, 100,000, 100,000,000?" Make eye contact with one person for each answer provided and use your arm to gesture to the whole group;

- Ask-and-answer—Ask a question of the whole group, pause, then answer it yourself, such as, "How many CEOs own stock in the corporations they manage? (Pause.) Would you believe __ percent?"

Avoid asking, "Are there any questions?" PLAN your questions and make them interesting to participants. Good questions help people understand and remember meeting content.

In answering questions from the audience, make sure they know there will be no ridicule or sarcasm in the answer. Never do or say anything to make questioners feel stupid or foolish. Ask for questions on specific statements or ideas just covered: "Do you have questions on step three of the implementation schedule?" If no one has a question, but there really should be some to avoid misunderstanding, say, "One of the most frequent questions at this stage is ____." Then the attendees understand that you really want them to ask questions. When you are asked a question, *repeat it* for the sake of those who didn't hear. This helps focus attention on the question and lets the questioner know the query is important.

Common answering mistakes include:

1. *Answering too much.* Keep answers short and concise. Long answers shut the attendees' responses down. The idea is for *them* to talk, not you.

2. *Answering too soon.* Interrupting speakers because you know what they are going to say is rude. Allow the group time to think of their responses. A pause or silence just says they are thinking about the question.

3. *Answering one person and continuing a dialogue.* The rest of the people lose interest when this goes on too long. Offer to talk further after the meeting, break eye contact, and move on.

Now that the leader role in decision making has been detailed, gaining consensus has been outlined, and questioning has been thoroughly considered, what else is needed in decision-making meetings? In problem solving, a problem is identified and analyzed. In decision making, criteria establishment is first, before leaders and groups can evaluate alternatives and decide on a plan of action. Implementation of the plan, assigning tasks and responsibilities, and scheduling will not be discussed here. These will vary considerably among organizations with different operating procedures.

Criteria Making

Remember the five alternatives produced in the problem-solving meeting? In the decision-making meeting, the goal is to decide which of these alternatives is the best of the five. Of course, the easiest way to do this is to put the five alternatives on an overhead, ask people to vote (majority rule), and that's that. The flaw here is not allowing for discussion and full understanding of the ramifications of each alternative—deliberation of these choices. So the end result here is *not* to race through this decision-making process just to get it done. It is to get everyone to consider each alternative carefully, giving special attention to the context of the situation, driving forces for and against, and who would be affected by each choice. Then, and only then, the group selects the best alternative. Leader behavior determines more crucially than in any other type of meeting the responses of people in the workforce at implementing decisions made here. Remember that meeting process determines outcome!

A better way to consider solutions to the problem outlined in the previous meeting is to create criteria with which to judge the effect of each alternative. As an example from the last chapter concerning saving adolescents, the alternatives created could be:

1. Educational institutions create school programs and scheduling better suited to adolescent development and interests.
2. Parents re-engage themselves with their young teens, offering more hands-on guidance, rules, and family activities.
3. Employers provide family-friendly policies: parental leave, and so on.
4. Youth organizations expand to reach out to this age group; organizations should be sanctioned by parents, schools, and communities.
5. The media is held more responsible for promoting better role models and "good kids," rather than glamourizing violence, sex, and drugs.

The meeting objective is: to choose the most acceptable way to meet the needs of young adolescents. (Other objectives possible: Which alternative to implement first or which alternative is most doable in our community, given its resources and other factors.)

Criteria usually concern:

- whose acceptance would be needed to implement an alternative;
- whether sponsoring organizations would accept the responsibility;
- the time required to implement the alternative;
- the cost of maintaining a program once established;
- the long- or short-term effectiveness of the alternative;
- the audience or market reached by the alternative if implemented
- the cost/benefit ratio;
- the number of personnel needed to carry out the alternative;
- the amount of time required from volunteers;
- the coordination required between institutions and other contributors.

Of course, this list names just a few considerations for criteria, but it's a start. Try not to use feasibility as a criterion, since it's a vague term that gives an overall approach, rather than specific concerns reflected in this list. The key for developing good criteria is to be as specific as possible. Envision the situation, then think of all the people affected by the problem, then think of what community resources exist or organizational resources could be tapped to address the problem.

For the purpose of this example, use any of the following:

Implementation time	Cost/benefit ratio
Responsible organization acceptance	Parental acceptance
Young adolescent acceptance	Long-term effectiveness
Openness to influence/public pressure	Coordination required

In effect, think about everything it would take to carry out these alternatives. The trick is to find criteria that apply to ALL the alternatives. If a criterion will only apply to one or two of your alternatives, it won't be useful in distinguishing between the alternatives. (Don't use feasibility!) Also distinguish clearly between your criteria. Using "time to implement" and "cost to implement" puts heavy attention on implementation questions, rather than the issue being considered. Choose criteria from separate areas of concern as much as possible; it makes for clearer information processing. If, indeed, a criterion is worthy of being considered more seriously or should be given more weight in deliberation, ask the participants to double the numbers they assign to that particular criterion.

Returning to the example of neglect of adolescents, make a grid for the alternatives and supply space for write-in criteria. Let the group select criteria from the list provided or from their own ideas.

Present this grid to participants in some way: overhead transparency, flipchart, posterboard, chalkboard, whiteboard, whatever; just create it before your meeting.

Meeting Objective: To choose the most acceptable way to meet the needs of young adolescents (10–14 years old)

Alternatives   **Totals**

Better school programs/scheduling						
Parents re-engage with teens						
Employers make family-friendly fix						
Expanded youth organizations						
Media promote good, not bad						

Legend: 1   2   3   4   5

$\longleftarrow \qquad\qquad\qquad \longrightarrow$

Acceptable   *Unacceptable*

It's also good to have it on your meeting agenda, something each person can see clearly and work with. Then have the group choose criteria for these alternatives. Meeting leaders need to consider criteria ahead of time and possibly make up a list as has been done in this example. However, it's important to include meeting attendees in the selection process. Let them think of criteria to use here as well. Ask them to vote as a group or have different people select one criteria or have them eliminate criteria from a list provided—make a group decision as to which criteria to use. Have the Recorder write in their selections, like this:

Meeting Objective: To choose the most acceptable way to meet the needs of young adolescents (10–14 years old)

Alternatives	Parental Acceptance	Young Adolescent Acceptance	Openness to Influence	Cost/Benefit Ratio	Implementation Time	Totals
Better school programs/ scheduling						
Parents re-engage with teens						
Employers make family-friendly fix						
Expanded youth organizations						
Media promote good, not bad						

Legend: 1   2   3   4   5

←——————————————————————————————→

Acceptable   *Unacceptable*

In this example, then, the group is looking for the one alternative which parents and young adolescents are most willing to accept, the one in which the organization named is open to influence or pressure, the one in which the cost of the alternative is acceptable in terms of the benefits, and the one which could be implemented most quickly.

Meeting leaders should summarize this selection for the group and ask them once again if these are the most important things they want to weigh in considering the alternatives. If the answer is yes, then remind them of the legend and ask them to assign a number as a vote for the alternative, given the criteria under consideration. For example, do participants think that parents would accept "better school programs or scheduling?" If so, enter a 1; if not, enter a 5; if maybe so, maybe not, enter a 2, 3, or 4, depending on the strength of belief. Then, ask whether young adolescents would accept better programs/scheduling; if so, enter 1 or 2; if not, enter 4 or 5, and so on. Then continue by asking whether schools would be open to influence or pressure from the public. Then ask if better programs or scheduling would be most beneficial in terms of costs to maintain these programs. Then ask how long it presumably would take to implement the programs/scheduling; enter a number to indicate an acceptable or unacceptable time length.

Proceed to the next alternative "parents re-engaging with teens." Remember that this will take time and effort on the part of parents—time away from work, effort to set up rules (like curfew) and carry through with these, scheduling family meals and time together. If parents are likely to accept this alternative, enter 1, and so on. Would young teens accept being more involved with their parents? Would parents be open to carry out this family change? Would the cost to parents be worth the benefit to family? How long would this take to implement?

Keep going through the alternatives with the perspective of each criterion in mind. Going across the grid is usually faster for groups, but going down is also fine to do. Ask groups to add up the totals going across to find their most acceptable alternative. Adding by going down will show the response to each criterion. Meeting leaders might want to ask groups, especially, which alternative was first choice and which criterion was most important to them. If the meeting format is ordinary group or nominal group, have individuals tell which alternative is their choice and which criterion was most important. This information tells meeting leaders what underlying concerns may be present among the participants. Also, if there are disparities in numbering, leaders should make sure these are differences of opinion, not rating errors. In groups, for example, the group recorder could enter a 1 when the group registered a 5, or the group may have gotten confused and voted the opposite of what they felt. This numbering system should produce areas for discussion as groups or individuals compare their thinking and voting.

Which alternative in the example will win? Probably the expanded youth organizations, given the criteria selected. Parents would like these, pre-teens certainly would like them since they'd have more opportunity to be with friends and form new friendships, plus explore their possibilities or developing interests. Youth organizations could be readily influenced. The cost may be a significant factor, but if the community sees a difference in young teens' behaviors or attitudes, any cost might be worth the expense. Plus civic organizations could share the expense through sponsoring youth organizations. Implementation time could be shorter with youth group expansion than with schools offering different programs or employers changing policies or sending media an effective message. An added benefit of youth group expansion is that parental involvement might be increased as well, structuring time between preteens and parents.

Meeting leaders need to draw out this information from participants in discussions by asking questions and having a clear sense of where the meeting is *likely* to end up. Even though the outcome isn't predictable, leaders can have a fair idea about how the selection process will turn out, through assessing the alternatives themselves and considering the context in which the meeting takes place. For example, affluent communities might select the most expensive alternative since money might not be an obstacle for them, whereas poorer communities might favor more of a let's-all-pitch-in-to-help, less money oriented choice, like parents re-engaging or asking employers for concessions. All this adds to discussion, and that's a major purpose in decision-making meetings!

Meeting success also depends on good criteria. Here are some examples.

Meeting Objective: To find the best way to make people aware of heart disease and heart attack

Alternatives	Acceptance of Sponsoring Institutions	Overall Effectiveness	Cost to Maintain Program	High School/ College Acceptance	Audience Reached	Totals
Educate the young						
Health club incentive plan						
Warning signs on high-fat food						
Seminars for college students						
Internet messages/ brochures						

Legend: 1   2   3   4   5

Acceptable ⟵——————————————————⟶ Unacceptable

Meeting Objective: To decide the best way to curb teenage smoking

Alternatives	Prevention Cost/Benefits	Short-Term Effectiveness	Adult/Parent Participation Needed	Acceptance of Teens	Market Size Reached	Totals
Educate teens in health classes						
Encourage joining school clubs						
Punish illegal sales to teens						
Celebrities promote no smoking						
"Scared straight" convocations						

Legend: Rating: 1 = workable   5 = unworkable

⟵——————————————————⟶
(any numbers in between OK to use)

Outline for Decision-Making Meeting

Opening
Show some pizzazz here! Give an opener that focuses interest in the topic. Reintroduce yourself, Facilitator, and Recorder. (1 min.)

Background
Give a good review of your topic here. Go through the first and second meetings, summarizing the content. OK to reshow overheads used then. Why listen to the topic? (WIIFM). (3 min.) Go over alternatives from problem solving, explaining them or expanding on them. Let us absorb your ideas again. (3–4 min.)

Preview
Tell the meeting plan you have. Are we going to separate into groups? Will we represent different factions? Will we write stuff on the board or do you have a different way to report numbers? (Poster board, transparencies, BIG paper, etc.) Are we ranking or rating? Will your Recorder and Facilitator collect numbers or will we do this by group report? Do you want a group representative to come up to the front to talk about group decisions, since people pay more attention this way? (2 min.)

Body
Select criteria. Have some criteria up your sleeve to fill in the blanks if the audience doesn't respond. Having some criteria already written is OK, but ask group for more. *No matter how you plan to gather the numbers, put your grid on the agenda.* People need something in their hands when matching criteria and alternatives. Have Recorder write in criteria selected. Then start your discussion plan: ordinary group, small group, nominal group, whatever. If small groups are used, give all instructions before anyone moves. (5 min.)

When the numbers start coming in, question big differences between numbers (3-point differences on a scale of 5). Ask groups/people to explain their thinking. Ask if groups/people want to change their numbers after a brief discussion. *Lead the discussion.* (5 min.)

When all the numbers are in, talk to the groups to see what each thought was the best alternative and which criterion was most important for them. Do this while your Recorder and Facilitator are adding up numbers. *Don't stand there watching the Recorder and Facilitator work!* You're in a meeting with the whole group! Ask a question, ask people to share their views, talk to them! (2 min.)

When the best alternative emerges, ask if the alternative makes sense as a solution to the problem posed. If it doesn't, ask people to explain and perhaps select another alternative. If two alternatives tie, work out a solution combining them. Also ask which criterion was most important and why. Scout for underlying truths. (3 min.)

Conclusion
Briefly track the content of all three meetings and the meeting objective and alternative chosen in this meeting. Then *give a close to remember!* Bring home one more time the importance of your topic. Last chance! (1–2 minutes)

No one likes to attend boring meetings! Be creative in planning and conducting this one. If everyone else uses small groups, use ordinary group or nominal group. A large sheet of paper across the front of the room serves as a useable grid, or put up posters for small groups and have the Recorder and Facilitator take in numbers for you on a master transparency. Have groups record their numbers on preprinted transparencies. Hand out treats! Give groups costumes to wear! Appeal to their sense of fun!

Comparing Alternatives

Announce the meeting objective; usually it is "to choose the best way to (do whatever the problem-solving meeting objective was)." Create several criteria and ask the group to add to the list (but think of several more just in case!). Make a list on the board or the overhead and provide the list of alternatives as well, so attendees can see both at the same time. Putting a grid on the agenda solves this problem. Then ask the group to select five criteria to use in making this decision. Why five? The time frame for this meeting is 25 to 30 minutes, and five alternatives measured against five criteria is about all anyone can accomplish. The criteria can be selected by hand vote, by polling people selected from the group, by voice vote—whatever method works.

When participants have supplied and selected the criteria they want to work with, have your Recorder put them in the grid. Ask people to write the criteria in the individual grids on the agenda, taking care to record the criteria in the right order—one agreeing with the master grid. Then, reveal your meeting plan to the participants. They will appreciate knowing exactly what they are to do when in the plan.

If factions or constituents with different perspectives on the problem exist, consider forming these into small groups which could, of course, vote in their own best interests. For example, if you're considering how to reform the welfare system, recipients of welfare funds would have different views from middle-class taxpayers, and both should have a say in the solution. Some groups will cancel each other out with their voting, but that's expected. The alternative chosen by both groups may be truly good!

In the example of neglected adolescents, a leader could ask one small group to represent parents, one to represent preteens themselves, one to represent employers, one for the media, and one for sponsors of youth organizations. Encourage groups to keep their particular mindset in operation during their deliberations. For example, if you were a preteen, do you think your parents or parents in general would accept better school programs and scheduling? If you were a preteen, would you accept this? As a preteen, do you think schools would be open to offering different programs and schedules? As a preteen, compare the cost of change to the benefits you could see. How long do you think it would take?

The idea of representation here is to ensure that all sides are heard. Consider asking each group to make a position statement to the others prior to voting. To make this fun, give the preteens lollipops. Make headbands with wrinkles drawn on them to depict the furrowed brows of parents. Tee shirts or paper sashes with names of youth organizations, ties or hard hats (or paper replicas) for employers, and press cards or toy cameras for the media would add to the spirit of the discussion.

Through the Legend, tell the group what numbering system you are using. For example, is 1 good and 5 bad or is 5 good and 1 bad? Also tell them whether you are rating or ranking. *Rating* means you can put any number to any alternative and have as many 2s or 4s or 5s as needed to express strength of opinion. *Ranking* means you have to assign 1 to one alternative only and 5 to another and then fill in with 2, 3, and 4. Put this information on an overhead or the board, so folks don't get confused.

Once again, what you are doing is asking the participants to consider each alternative in light of each criteria and assigning a number to signify agreement-disagreement, acceptability-unacceptability, and so on. The numbers chosen represent the degree or strength of conviction concerning the alternative and criterion. If the plan is to divide into groups, give complete instructions to the whole group before anyone moves. Once chairs start scraping and people seek out other group members, leaders can be drowned out in the noise. Folks usually aren't listening anyway at that point.

NOW, start carrying out the plan for discussion and voting. Either divide into small groups or use ordinary group format or nominal groups and ask them to assign numbers to each alternative from the standpoint of each criterion. Remember to include a legend wherever the grid is displayed. (Pluses and minuses usually don't work well, since it's hard to add and subtract them.)

YOUR ROLE IS TO RUN THE MEETING, NOT DO EVERYTHING YOURSELF!

After groups have finished their work, you, your Facilitator, and/or your Recorder take the numbers each group has come up with and put them in a grid on an overhead transparency, a poster, a BIG sheet of paper, something the whole group can see easily. *Use a Recorder and Facilitator in this meeting.* Common procedure is to have Facilitator and Recorder take in the numbers while you listen for discrepancies, like when one group gives a 5 and another gives a 1. You should stop the action and ask what their thinking was, so all can understand why the numbers varied so. Number differences of more than *three* deserve discussion. Ask groups, after they've listened to others' thinking, whether they want to change their numbers. Sometimes participants get numbers confused or the group recorder makes an error, so make sure the group didn't make a mistake with numbering.

After all the shouting is over and the numbers are on the grid, *ask the whole group* to select the "winner." Then ask if this makes sense in terms of the original meeting objective. This step is not the equivalent of spitting in the wind! Sometimes numbers don't produce a logical choice. If this is true, ask if the group wants to consider another alternative or if they wish to combine some. If time permits, talk briefly about how to implement the alternative.

Summarize BRIEFLY the information meeting, the problem solving meeting, the meeting objective for this meeting and the alternative selected as winner. Then close the meeting. Put some artfulness or cleverness in this. It's your last chance to remind the group of the importance of the topic. Saying thanks and sitting down abruptly isn't "good theatre." Meeting leaders work long and hard to get to this point. Glory in it!

MEETING EVALUATION FORM

Directions: Rate each item on a scale of 1-5, with 1 indicating a need for improvement, 3 indicating adequate performance, and 5 optimum performance.

_____ Did everyone participate?
_____ Did the discussion stay on track?
_____ Did we stick to the time schedule?
_____ Did the meeting make good use of attendees' abilities?
_____ Was the meeting leader effective as a discussion coordinator?
_____ Were disagreements resolved smoothly?
_____ What was the quality of the decision we made?
_____ Was the stated purpose of the meeting achieved?
_____ Did the meeting manager's team function well together?
_____ Was the meeting fun?
_____ TOTAL

(Adapted, Lippincott, 1994, p. 118)

AGENDA FOR DECISION-MAKING MEETING

Meeting Objective:

Logistics	Meeting Members
Date:	1. Leader:
Time:	2. Attendees:
Location:	Meeting called by:
	Phone:

Agenda Item	Process	Time	Who's Responsible

DECISION-MAKING MEETING CRITIQUE

LEADER: **OBSERVER:**   **PTS. POSSIBLE: 60**

PREPARATION:

Professional appearance   (3) _____

Quality & use of visual aids   (3) _____

Detailed agenda   (3) _____

PRESENTATION:

OPENING: Reintroduce self & general topic   (1) _____

BACKGROUND: Describe the problem; WIIFM   (5) _____

               Review five alternatives   (3) _____

PREVIEW: Session organization & what you expect
               people to do   (2) _____

BODY: *Lead group* in setting up criteria
               (5 criteria minimum)   (5) _____

               Lead group in comparing alternatives with
               criteria (5 alternatives minimum)   (10) _____

               Lead group in selecting the best alternative;
               determine which criterion was most important (5) _____

CONCLUSION: Review previous meetings & reiterate
               meeting objective & alternative chosen   (5) _____

               Close meeting   (3) _____

PERFORMANCE:

Time management (25-30 minutes)   (3) _____

Vitality/leadership   (3) _____

Use of Recorder and Facilitator   (3) _____

Creativity; maintaining interest in topic   (3) _____

TOTAL POINTS EARNED

Comments:

OBSERVATION SHEET
for Decision-Making Meeting

PRESENTER: _____   OBSERVER: _____

5—Excellent   4—Good   3—Average   2—Needs work   1—Poor

PERSONAL PREPARATION

1. Appropriate business attire	5	4	3	2	1
2. Voice quality/tone	5	4	3	2	1
3. Voice audibility	5	4	3	2	1
4. Confidence displayed	5	4	3	2	1

PRESENTATION PREPARATION

5. Good organization	5	4	3	2	1
6. Meaningful topic/key point development	5	4	3	2	1
7. Attention-getting opening/closing	5	4	3	2	1
8. Easy-to-follow delivery	5	4	3	2	1
9. Rehearsed performance	5	4	3	2	1

PROJECTION

10. Vocal effectiveness (intonation, fillers, pauses)	5	4	3	2	1
11. Audience interaction/eye contact	5	4	3	2	1
12. Energy/enthusiasm portrayed	5	4	3	2	1

STRONG POINTS: WORK ON:

| DECISION-MAKING MEETING |
| SELF-CRITIQUE/SINGLE CONFERENCE REPORT |

Name:

General topic:

Decision-making meeting objective:

Please type your answers to these questions. Be aware that these are open-ended questions intended for discussion, rather than "Oh, yes, I did that" answers. (Brevity is good, but pithy conciseness is beautiful.)

1. After watching your video, comment on the visual impression you give. Do you look/act like you're truly leading this meeting?

2. How well did the group understand your instructions for organizing your session? (Did they start to work immediately with little further instruction from you or did they look blank for a while and then ask what to do?) What could you have done differently?

3. In comparing alternatives with the criteria, what did you find most difficult to do? Did you get frustrated trying to get others to agree?

4. Was your summary complete and memorable?

5. What are the major gains you've made in presenting information and conducting meetings, as evidenced in this videotape?

FINAL CONFERENCE REPORT

Directions: Watch your videotaped conferences from beginning to end and respond to the questions asked. Title your responses after the main headings provided in these questions. Papers are expected to have appropriate wording, spelling, grammar, and expression.

IMPROVING

1. Look at all three grading sheets for your conferences and list two major items you needed to improve. You may also use verbal feedback given at your meetings. What did you do to improve each of these? (2 pts.)

THINKING ON YOUR FEET

2. Basically, this instruction improves the skill of thinking on your feet (TOYF). (Definition of thinking on your feet: processing information and transforming it into something useful in "real time," immediately.) Don't include your lack of planning:
"I forgot to plan an opener, so I just made one up on the spot." TOYF is, "I dropped all my note cards and gave my talk from memory." Give three instances in which you had to TOYF during your conferences. (6 pts.)

CHOOSING TOPICS

3. List the topic you chose and comment honestly on whether it was a wise choice. Why or why not? List two other good topics. (2 pts.)

CONDUCTING MEETINGS

4. How important do you think it is to learn to present information and conduct problem-solving and decision-making meetings? Have you used these skills in other settings? Comment on the value of creating criteria for making decisions. (4 pts.)

Further directions: Create a cover sheet for this report. Include this:

FINAL CONFERENCE REPORT

by

(Your name)
(Class time)

In partial completion
of the requirements for
(Class title)

(Month, year)

References

Arredondo, L. 1994. *The McGraw-Hill 36-hour course: Business presentations*. NY: McGraw-Hill.

Arredondo, L. 1991. *How to present like a pro: Getting people to see things your way*. NY: McGraw-Hill.

Carnegie Council on Adolescent Development. 1995. *Great transitions: Preparing adolescents for a new century*. NY: Carnegie Corporation of New York.

Chang, R. Y., and K. R. Kehoe. 1994. *Meetings that work*. Irvine, CA: Richard Chang Associates.

D'Arcy, J. 1992. *Technically speaking*. NY: American Management Association.

Doyle, M., and D. Straus. 1993. *How to make meetings work*. NY: Berkley Books.

Hyman, R. T. 1980. *Improving discussion leadership*. NY: Teachers College Press.

Johnson, D. W., & Johnson, F. P. (1997). *Joining together: Group theory and group skills*. Boston: Allyn and Bacon.

Kushner, M. 1997. *Successful presentations for dummies*. Indianapolis, IN: IDG Books Worldwide.

Lewin, K. 1951. Field theory in social science. NY: Harper.

Lippincott, S. M. 1994. *Meetings: Dos, don'ts and donuts: The complete handbook for successful meetings*. Pittsburgh, PA: Lighthouse Point Press.

Miller, R. F. 1997. *Running a meeting that works*. 2nd ed. Hauppauge, NY: Barron's Educational Series.

Peoples, D. A. 1992. *Presentations plus*. 2nd ed. NY: Wiley.

Tropman, J. E. 1996. *Making meetings work: Achieving high quality group decisions*. Thousand Oaks, CA: Sage Publications.

Appendix

Presentation Materials

MEETING MANAGEMENT

40 to 60% of managerial workdays spent in meetings

7 to 15% of personnel budgets spent on meetings

"Recruiting Trends"

Annual Report
Collegiate Employment Institute
Michigan State University

College grads need:

Public speaking and presentation skills

Complex critical thinking skills

Solid communication abilities

Computer aptitude

Leadership and teamwork skills

Survey: 320 employers nationwide in manufacturing, finance, and professional services

Meetings

Effective way to accomplish tasks in organizations
Encourage togetherness, trust, and a sense of belonging

Increased commitment to organization
Improved decision quality

Scheduled time together for work groups
Morale effect in organizations
Productivity gain

Image enhancement for meeting leaders

Types of Meetings

INFORMATION MEETING

Presentation skills

Structuring information for delivery

Writing a meeting objective

Constructing a meeting agenda

PROBLEM-SOLVING MEETING

Meeting roles

Planning for interactive meetings

Influencing groups

Conducting discussions

DECISION-MAKING MEETING

Meeting disruptions

Framing decisions

Establishing criteria

Questioning techniques

Achieving consensus

To persuade people, relate to them!

- *Understand their points of view to "see" how they might accept your point of view*

- *Think from the other side of your desk*

- *Consider your listeners'*

ages and genders

levels of education

jobs/professions

expectations

AGENDAS

MEETING OBJECTIVE
What do I want people to do during this meeting?
Be specific & concise
Use action verbs (things you can see people doing)
Determine the content of the meeting at the appropriate level of detail

LOGISTICS
Where, when, what to bring
Who should attend
Who called the meeting, phone/email

PROCESS
Method for dealing with agenda item:
smaller group discussion, interactive lecture, brainstorming?

Most important part of preparing for meetings

Structuring a topic

PREPARING   PRESENTING

INTRO:	Opener
	Introduce you
	Meeting objective
	(Introduce you)
	Preview
BODY:	Three key points
	Supporting material
	Transitions
CLOSING:	Summary
	To-do statement

Objective

Key points

Supporting material

Transition statements

Preview and summary

Opening

Closing

Dumb things meeting leaders do

Poor first impression

Dull, dry, boring delivery

Frozen in one spot

Deadpan facial expression

Weak eye contact

No audience involvement

Inaudible voice

Poor visual aids

Inept use of visual aids

COMMUNICATION DELIVERY CUES
Dr. Albert Mehrabian studying face-to-face communication

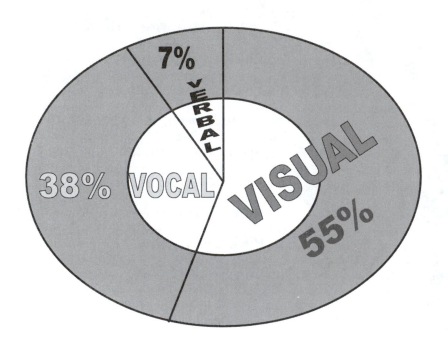

NONVERBAL COMMUNICATION

CHARISMA / PRESENCE

poise
bearing
facial expressions
body movements
posture

EMOTIONAL EXPRESSIVITY

positive emotions
emotional ties to audience
liking, caring
concern for feelings
reassuring, comforting

Most important?

YOUR EYES

Look at people directly to make them
feel you understand them and want
the best for them

YOUR VOICE

Must be projected
Supported by the diaphragm
Rate
Pitch
Inflection
Articulation
Fillers

Shows feelings, attitudes, physical state, self image

tips

Good content can't save bad delivery
Prepare and PRACTICE
Use your hand, palm up, to call on people
Tune into station WIIFM
Fill the room with your presence
Convince people you care

Why have meetings?

- *different people bring different resources—experiences, knowledge*
- *implementation easier when people participate in decision making*
- *togetherness and trust bring renewed commitment to organizations*
- *connectedness, sense of community add to feeling of comradery*
- *powerful way to change people's minds and behaviors*

*Best way to communicate when what **YOU** say depends on what **OTHERS** say*

What's wrong with meetings?

No reason to meet

Poor meeting process

Lack of standards

Poor preparation

Lack of information

Better way to do things

Secret to success:

Knowing

that meeting PROCESS

determines OUTCOME

Meeting approaches

group centered

Problem-solving meetings
Decision-making meetings
Small group meetings

More difficult for leader
More interaction and emotions
See others' viewpoints
Better decisions
People feel better when they talk

More time needed
Discussion must be controlled
Meaningful exchange managed

LEADER RUNS THE SHOW

leader controlled

Information-giving meetings
Large group meetings

Easy for the leader
Much information in short time
Few surprises

No free flow of information
Sensitive issues don't emerge
All people aren't heard

LEADER IS THE SHOW

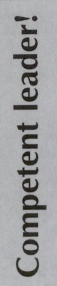

Competent leader!

Cut through chaos to find issues that matter

Get people to deliberate issues

Lead decision making on issues

Meeting Cost$

Names of attendees

Time Value: hourly pay or
               % of salary / # of work days per year

Multiply time value by length of your meeting

Add preparation costs:
       handouts/visuals, room costs, refreshments,
       transportation, guest speaker

Total   =   Meeting costs

WELL-PLANNED WELL-EXECUTED MEETINGS

PRODUCE BETTER RESULTS IN SHORTER TIME FRAMES

ARE MOST COST EFFECTIVE

MUST BE CONNECTED WITH "BOTTOM LINE"
decreased operating expense
hourly wages saved
productivity gain
managerial hours saved

MUST BE DOCUMENTED (FOR YOUR PAY RAISE/PROMOTION)

Recorder

Keep track of meeting action

Capture the idea using key words & phrases

Write only when & what the Leader says to write

Capture words expressed, not your interpretation

Check with Leader & Facilitator for accuracy

Ask for help if note keeping is slowing down the meeting

Participants

Be on time
Follow ground rules

Participate fully in discussions
No social loafing

Listen to others without rushing to judgment
Avoid causing meeting distractions

Facilitator

Direct discussion traffic
"Everyone clear on directions?" "Have you finished? OK, it's your turn to talk."
Command the attention of the group
"Let's have everyone's attention up here, please." "Are you thinking or asleep?"

Ensure participation
"You're doing great. Let's keep going!" (Silent person), "What do you think?"
Restart when things go wrong
"Looks like we're bogged down. Let's go back a step and refocus."

Remain neutral
"As Facilitator, I can't give you an opinion."
Protect people from verbal attacks
"Let's keep the language clean." "Let's focus on the topic, not personalities."

Leader

Start and end on time
Use your agenda

Use ground rules if necessary
Create a cordial, businesslike atmosphere
Tell Recorder what to write; tell Facilitator what to do

Restate questions asked; paraphrase to ensure understanding
Participate in discussions; state your opinions

Change the meeting format if necessary
Summarize key decisions and actions

SILENT PERSONS

Stand close to them

Call them by name

Ask them questions

Ask them to put away reading material

On break, ask why they aren't talking

SHY PERSONS

Make eye contact & smile

Ask an open question

Thank them for response

Ask them to summarize

Ask all to share opinions

On break, talk to them; encourage them

Whisperers

Side Conversationalists

Make eye contact
Stand near them
Stop meeting; maintain silence

"Would you like to share your ideas?"
"Shall we add what you're discussing to the agenda?"

Talkalots

Know it alls

Hostiles

Loudmouths

Loudmouths

"Would you take notes?"

"What was your question?"

"Hold that thought; let Jennifer finish."

"What's your point?"

"Sorry, we're out of time."

"Thanks for your comments."

"I'd like to hear from others."

"How does that relate to this topic?"

Know it alls

Stick to facts you know

Cite other authority figures and their statements

Ask them to serve as references during the meeting.

Avoid eye contact and don't call on them.

Defuse the situation: state his point of view and tell why you disagree.

"We recognize your experience here, but everyone has a say in this."

"Those are some of the problems; do you have any solutions?"

"I think we understand your point of view; let's hear from others."

Hostiles

Don't get defensive
Don't argue with them

Don't lecture / threaten them
Don't criticize or shame them

Don't tell them where to go
Don't ask them to leave

Ask people to keep an open mind; defuse
Ask another member of the audience to respond

Clean up Hostile's words
Agree to disagree & discuss after meeting

Find one point to agree with & move on
Ask for solutions to problems/statements

Call time
Avoid eye contact; don't call on them

DO

call a meeting when:

- you want information or advice

- you want help solving a problem

- an issue impacts the organization

- problems exist between groups

- you or the groups want to meet

DON'T

call group meetings when you:

- have made the decision already

- can contact the group a better way

- don't have time to prepare to meet

- don't have enough information

- need to hire, fire, discuss salary, or evaluate employees

Meetings function as information-processing systems

In GOOD meetings:

1. *issues are fully discussed*

2. *decisions are well considered need no rework*

3. *attendees enjoy meeting feel good about participating*

- *a social activity*

- *a cooperative effort of group members studying a problem*

- *a purposeful interchange*

- *a systematic progression toward a goal*

- *a creative verbal interchange as people listen and respond*

- *a focused activity requiring leadership*

- *a full expression of differing viewpoints*

- *a reflective thinking activity (pros and cons, alternatives, consequences of actions)*

LEADER ROLE IN DISCUSSION

✔ *Clarify the question before the group—*
   the meeting objective

✔ *Decide and explain the structure for*
   the discussion

✔ *Conduct the discussion*
   Draw out people's opinions
   Encourage responses from all
   Repeat responses so all can hear
   Summarize each key idea or point

✔ *Ask group to reach conclusions based on*
   meeting content

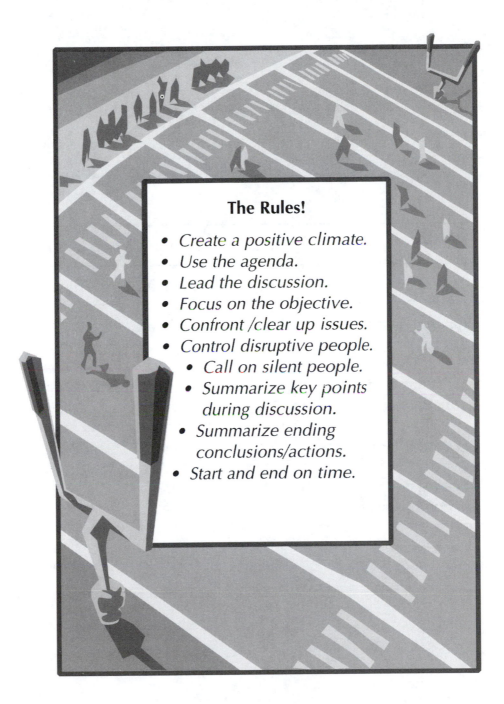

The Rules!

- Create a positive climate.
- Use the agenda.
- Lead the discussion.
- Focus on the objective.
- Confront /clear up issues.
- Control disruptive people.
  - Call on silent people.
  - Summarize key points during discussion.
  - Summarize ending conclusions/actions.
- Start and end on time.

Discussion Techniques

Criteria	Ordinary	Brainstorming	Nominal
Number of ideas	**low**	**moderate**	high
Quality of ideas	**low**	**moderate**	high
Social pressure	high	**low**	**moderate**
Time/money costs	**moderate**	low	low
Potential for conflict	high	**low**	**moderate**
Feelings of accomplishment	high/**low**	high	high
Development of "we" feeling	high	high	**moderate**

Guiding Discussions

- *Establish a basis for discussion: review information*

- *Develop the discussion*

- *Ask for exchanges of agreement or disagreement*

- *Summarize key points*

- *Summarize ending conclusions; get group agreement*

- *Specify future actions stemming from discussion*

Develop the Discussion

- *two people with pro & con views*

- *prepared statement with clarification questions*

- *each attendee responds to meeting objective*

- *role play to bring out different viewpoints*

- *create subgroups representing different viewpoints*

- *create subgroups; ask for positional statements/ recommendations/solutions*

then ask all to voice information and opinions

Facilitator's Role

1. Manages the meeting <u>process</u> so that Leader is free to manage meeting <u>content</u>;

2. Listens for discussion "drift;" refocuses on meeting purpose;

3. Deals with disruptive and inappropriate behavior;

4. Mediates conflicting opinions; does NOT voice own opinions;

5. Suggests other approaches when one isn't working;

6. Monitors time spent on agenda items;

7. Takes directions from Leader.

- Provide needed information; correct errors

- Offer new ways to view problems

- Offer mini-summaries from time to time

- Clarify points and reflect the impact of remarks

- Restate views of others to check understanding

- Find merit in others' ideas

- Ask questions to help others express thoughts

- Focus on meeting objective/point of discussion

- Exclude ideas that do not add to discussion

- Make progress in discussions

- State your viewpoint and listen to others'

- Remain calm and reasonable in exchanges

- Summarize group conclusions; seek agreement

- Determine further actions/implementation

ROLE OF THE RECORDER

— *Keep a visual record of the meeting*

— *Write what people actually say, not your words*

— *Use key words and phrases, not sentences*

— *Check with Leader for accuracy*

— *Write only what Leader says to write*

— *Ask for help if recording slows meeting progress*

— *Record overhead/chalkboard content for Leader*

— *Construct meeting minutes if asked*

Summarizing the Discussion

~ **Recapitulate key points of the discussion**

~ **Define areas of agreement/disagreement**

~ **Synthesize major ideas**

~ **Express minority opinions**

~ **Avoid adding personal perspectives**

~ **Ask for/state future activities—to do statement**

~ **Compliment group for good discussion**

~ **Close the meeting**

Advantages of Group Decision Making

Common thoughts

Blind spot recognition

Unique ideas

Accurate recall

Commitment to implementation

People's ideas/experiences

Process gain

Social facilitation

DISCUSSION

Changes attitudes and behaviors

Encourages verbal commitment to new behaviors

Provides social support and cooperation for changing

Authoritative style appropriate when:

- decisions don't require commitment of group

- coordination of group activity is simple and easy

- decisions must be made quickly

CONSENSUS

Group solidarity in sentiment and belief

- Allow time for all to state their views
- Ensure understanding of all views
- Encourage opposing viewpoints
- Clarify reasoning and information for viewpoints
- When differences occur, clarify issues and gather information
- Discourage "giving in" just to avoid conflict
- Arrive at a decision all can support
- Create a sense of gain, not loss

Asking questions

Probing to get at ideas

Supporting people when they talk

Listening as people talk

GOAL

QUESTIONS TO ASK

To get information

Begin with "what, where, when, why, who, how."

To broaden discussion

How would you do that?
What should we think about?

To verify information

Where did you hear that?
Have you tried this?

To test assumptions

What would happen if we tried this?

To voice your opinion

Would this idea work?
Would you try this?

To reach agreement

Which plan do we like?
Which idea can we all support?
Do we all agree this is what we want?

PROBING QUESTIONS

SUPPORTING

Encourage participation from silent/shy people
Praise people for words/actions
Relieve tension with humor

Make eye contact
Smile
Listen

Focus discussion on someone's response

LISTENING

Face speakers

Hear speakers out and check for understanding

Clarify by asking questions

Rephrase and ask if restatement is correct

Put what's said into your own words

Questioning techniques

Less than 30:

Name Response
Delayed name response
Boomerang
Back-at-you

More than 30:

Fill-in-the-blanks
Multiple choice
Ask-and-answer

Criteria making

What is the short or long-term effect of the alternative?

How many people would be required to implement the idea?
If volunteers are needed, how many or how much time is required?

How much coordination is required? How difficult would this be?
Would sponsoring organizations accept responsibility?

How much time would implementation take?
What market/audience would be reached?

Whose acceptance is needed?
What is the cost/benefit ratio?

Criteria making

Find criteria that apply to all alternatives

Distinguish clearly between criteria

Choose criteria from separate areas of concern

Assign more weight to more important criteria

Envision the situation, think of the people involved, the resources needed, and what it would take to carry out the alternatives.

MEETING EVALUATION

Scale: 1–5   1 = Needs improvement
               3 = Adequate
               5 = Optimum performance

_____ Did everyone participate?
_____ Did the discussion stay on track?
_____ Did we stick to the time schedule?
_____ Did the meeting make good use of attendees' abilities?
_____ Was the meeting leader effective as a discussion coordinator?
_____ Were disagreements resolved smoothly?
_____ What was the quality of the decision we made?
_____ Was the stated purpose of the meeting achieved?
_____ Did the meeting manager's team function well together?
_____ Was the meeting fun?

_____ **TOTAL**

Index